Working Together for Local Integration of Migrants and Refugees in Gothenburg

This document, as well as any data and any map included herein, are without prejudice to the status of or sovereignty over any territory, to the delimitation of international frontiers and boundaries and to the name of any territory, city or area.

Please cite this publication as:
OECD (2018), *Working Together for Local Integration of Migrants and Refugees in Gothenburg*, OECD Publishing, Paris.
http://dx.doi.org/10.1787/9789264299603-en

ISBN 978-92-64-29959-7 (print)
ISBN 978-92-64-29960-3 (PDF)

The statistical data for Israel are supplied by and under the responsibility of the relevant Israeli authorities. The use of such data by the OECD is without prejudice to the status of the Golan Heights, East Jerusalem and Israeli settlements in the West Bank under the terms of international law.

Photo credits: Cover © Marianne Colombani

Foreword

An OECD-EU initiative: "A territorial approach to migrant integration: The role of local authorities"

This publication on *Migrant Integration in Gothenburg* was produced by the OECD as part of a larger study on "A Territorial approach to migrant integration: The role of local authorities" supported by the European Commission

This study takes stock of the existing multi-level governance frameworks and policies for migrant and refugee integration at the local level in nine large European cities: Amsterdam, Athens, Barcelona, Berlin, Glasgow, Gothenburg, Paris, Rome and Vienna and a small city in Germany (Altena) thanks to the support of the German Ministry for Economic Affairs and Energy. It also builds on information collected from other 61 European cities, including Utrecht, through an ad-hoc survey and on a statistical database on migrant outcomes at regional (TL2) level. This study resulted in the **Working together for local integration of migrants and refugees Report**, approved by the OECD Committee for regional development policy (RDPC) in December 2017 (OECD, 2018[1]).

The focus of this study is on ''migrants'', meaning a wide range of different groups of people with different reasons for leaving their countries of origin: humanitarian, economic, family or study, among others. The target group includes newcomers, from EU and non-EU countries, as well as migrants who settled in the cities many years ago and native-born with at least one migrant parent,[1] depending on the statistical definition used by the city. Given the recent increase in the arrival of refugees and asylum seekers to Europe, particular attention is paid to these groups throughout the case studies.

Cities in the sample have different track records in integrating migrants. The study looks at updates to the governance mechanisms in the wake of the recent influx of asylum seekers and refugees, in order to improve the local reception of migrants and the capacity to integrate them into the society. Conversely, it also investigates opportunities to extend some of the services recently established for newcomers to long-standing migrant groups.

The point of departure for the overall study is the observation that in practice integration takes place at the local level. Cities are focal spots of refugee and migrant reception and integration processes: in 2015, close to two-thirds of the foreign-born population in the OECD lived in urban areas (OECD, 2018[1]).

The ambition of this series of case studies is to identify *how* cities have responded to these objectives. It aims to address an information vacuum: beyond the dominant literature on international and national evidence about migrant movements and integration, several studies exist about the local dimension and impact of migration.

1.See definition of migration given below.

However, they do not explore the governance factor attached to it. In the view of partner cities and international organisations (UNHCR, etc.), multi-level governance can be an important explanatory factor of the performance of migrant integration policies. Even though migration policies are the responsibility of the national government, the concentration of migrants in cities, and particularly in metropolitan areas (Brezzi et al., 2016), has an impact on the local demand for work, housing, goods and services that local authorities have to manage. Local authorities act within a multi-level budgetary and administrative framework, which limits or adds responsibilities in dealing with migrant-specific impacts in their territory. As such, this work first aims at understanding the way cities and their partners address migrant integration issues. While it DOESN'T strive at this stage to evaluate the impact of the whole set of local public actions, it compiles qualitative evidence of city policies, decision making and evaluation processes across selected multi-level governance dimensions. These dimensions were selected according to the multi-level governance gaps analysis developed by the OECD (Charbit, 2011; Charbit and Michalun, 2009). Statistical data have been collected from all of the cities on the presence and outcomes of migrant and refugee populations.

As a result of this comparative work, and in collaboration with partner cities and organisations, the OECD compiled a list of key objectives to guide policy makers in integrating migrants with a multi-level perspective. The ***Checklist for public action to migrant integration at the local level, as included in the Synthesis Report*** (OECD, 2018[1]) is articulated according to 4 blocks and 12 objectives. The four blocks cover: 1) institutional and financial settings; 2) time and proximity as keys for migrants and host communities to live together; 3) enabling conditions for policy formulation and implementation; and 4) sectoral policies related to integration: access to the labour market, housing, social welfare and health, and education.

This study first provides insight on the city's migration background and current situation. It then gives a description of the actions implemented following the framework of the "Checklist for public action to migrant integration at the local level".

The objective is to allow cities to learn from each other and to provide national and supranational decision makers and key partners of local integration policies with better evidence to address the major challenges ahead in this field and to adopt appropriate incentive schemes.

Acknowledgements

This publication "Working together for local integration of migrants and refugees: The case of Gothenburg" was produced by the OECD in partnership with the European Commission as part of a larger study on "Territorial approach to migrant integration: The role of local authorities".

This case study has been written by Anna Piccinni, Policy analyst, under the supervision of Claire Charbit, Head of the Territorial Dialogue and Migration Unit, within the Centre for Entrepreneurship, SMEs, Regions and Cities of the OECD. This report is based on substantive inputs and contributions by Helena Lindholm (external consultant, University of Gothenburg), Gaetan Muller (OECD) and Paola Proietti (OECD).

The case study has been realised thanks to the close collaboration of the Municipality of Gothenburg who provided the information and organised the OECD field work. The Secretariat would like to express its gratitude to all the participants to the interviews (see Annex 1). In particular to national government representatives and to the staff of the municipality, in particular to Pia Borg, Jackie Brown, Thomas Ekberg for their continuous support throughout the realisation of the case study. The secretariat would like to thank Ann-Sofie Hermansson, Chairwoman of Gothenburg municipal board, for her participation to this work.

This case study benefitted from the comments of other colleagues across OECD directorates: Lucie Cerna (EDU), Thomas Liebig (ELS/IMD), Antonella Noya (CFE), Rachel Scott (DCD) and Lisa Andersson (DEV).

The Secretariat is especially thankful for the financial contribution and the collaboration throughout the implementation of the project to the European Union Directorate General for Regional and Urban Policy. In particular we would like to thank Andor Urmos, Louise Bonneau and Judith Torokne-Rozsa for their guidance as well as for their substantive inputs during the revision of the case study.

Table of contents

Tables

Figures

Boxes

Executive summary

The population of Gothenburg is growing at a fast pace with 4,400 new residents registered in 2016 (Swedish Central Bureau of Statistics SCB) and more than 100 000 new jobs have been created since 2000 (Business Region Göteborg 2016). Newcomers account for the bulk of demographic growth. In fact, 12,858 refugees settled in the city between 2010 and 2016. Gothenburg, as the rest of Sweden experienced a peak in arrivals of refugees and asylum seekers in particular since 2012 and in particular in 2015 when 6 193 asylum seekers were hosted in the city (see section 1.1). However, migration is not a new phenomenon: 25% of the city's population are immigrants, 34% of the population has a migration background (i.e., themselves or at least one of their parents were born outside of Sweden) and 41.7% of the immigrants arrived more than 10 years ago and entered the country for humanitarian reasons. This is in line with Sweden's migration policy, which, since the 1970s, has focused primarily on safeguarding the right of asylum refugees and their families. Between 2004 and 2013, this segment of the population accounted for nearly 60% of permanent migrant inflows to Sweden (OECD, 2016b[2]). Consequently, national and local integration policies in Sweden address, for the most part, refugees and their families, which are also the focus of this study. The study is structured according to the 12 objectives identified in the OECD Checklist for public action to migrant and refugees integration at the local level, developed in 2017 through the joint OECD-EU project Territorial approach to migrant integration: the role of local authorities, which is included in the Synthesis Report (OECD, 2018[1])

Key Findings:

Some of the remaining challenges

Evaluations of the urban situation, which were undertaken by the municipality, have shown patterns of segregation and inequalities (Gothenburg, 2014[3]). A geographical, socio-spatial division has built up over time, where some districts are dominated by ''Swedes'' such as the Southwest and others are dominated by immigrants. It emerges that some of the neighbourhoods characterised by a high presence of ethnic minorities are also marked by low socio-economic outcomes in terms of income, education, life expectancy, trust, health, etc. (Gothenburg, 2014[3]).

It is generally assumed that housing and spatial segregation is the main obstacle to integration in Gothenburg. This issue includes the general shortage of housing as well as the structural organisation of the city in relation to space. Ambitious plans are underway, based on principles of social inclusion and sustainability. Until long-term housing plans are ready (see section 2.4.4), it is important that the city works towards decreasing segregation through short-term activities, for example distributing the responsibility for schooling refugees to more districts and working actively to assign newly arrived to housing in other parts of the city than the Northeast.

Closely connected to the housing situation is the segregation and unequal conditions across schools in Gothenburg (see section 2.4.4). Actions in a long-term perspective need to be taken, in order to foster heterogeneous schools and improve pupils' results. Through increased cooperation between districts in Gothenburg and between municipalities in the region on, for example, sharing the responsibility for the schooling of newly arrived children, achievements could be made. For instance, in Amsterdam newly arrived refugees and asylum seekers were distributed across 114 elementary and secondary schools.

More needs to be done in order to ease the paths into employment and efforts to match newly arrived with labour market demands. In addition, cooperation between the private sector and the Employment Agency needs to be encouraged. The private sector has an important role to play when it comes to employment, and more could be done in improving cooperation between the Municipality (the Integration Centre), the Västra Götaland Region, the Employment Agency and Business Region Göteborg. The Göteborg & co[1] platform between the private sector, municipality and university could be used as a model of working together around issues related to labour market inclusion between the municipality, other official agencies and actors, civil society organisations, the private sector and the two city universities.

The 2016 Asylum law (see Objective 4.3) reduced the visibility that status holders (in particular beneficiaries of subsidiary protection) have on the length of their stay. Employment Agency and other actors interviewed expressed concern about the effectiveness of the Introduction programme, given this reduced visibility.

According to testimonies from Civil Society Organisations (CSOs) involved in integration services in Gothenburg migrants can experience disruption in access to public services. This is due to a variety of reasons: swift changes in status and regulation, lack of up-to-date information about users' rights and procedures, obstacles to sharing administrative documents from one service to the other, silos approach in designing services for this public that doesn't allow for coherence across the policies offered (i.e. ensuring through services' coordination that a single and unemployed mother can leave her kids at school or kindergarten as long as she needs, in order to attend professional training or language classes). While the city doesn't adopt specific measures targeting migrant and refugee's access to services, the municipality could adopt a 'roadmap' approach, adopting the perspective of a migrant at the key turning points of his/her life (i.e. enrolling kids in school, access medical services, access social housing, organise family reunification, etc.). This 'roadmap approach' could allow that all departments check the compatibility of their policies and measures with migrant and refugee needs. In this sense, the city could benefit from the examples of the Start Wien office or the Berlin Pass as cross-sectoral solutions that offer the most vulnerable individuals integrated solutions to access services throughout their lives.

Coordination and dialogue with non-governmental organisations doesn't seem to happen on a regular basis with regard reception of newcomers and there is no platform for dialogue between the municipality and migrant communities. A more long term strategy to engage with NGOs could be instrumental for achieving the road map approach. Thanks to their expertise NGOs could complement cities services where refugees need accompaniment until the point they can access to universal services autonomously. In this sense, the mechanisms for coordination put in place in Barcelona and Athens with regard to migrant and refugee issues can held up as best practices to be replicated elsewhere.

What is already done and how it could be improved

Local Vision on migrants and refugees integration: The guiding principle for national and local administration is that public services are accessible to all groups on the same basis. Therefore there are no national 'integration code' or city integration strategy. However, concerned by sustainability and the level of inequalities, the city has formulated 30 proposals for "reducing inequality in living conditions and creating good opportunities in life for everyone" (see section 2.1.2). The intention of equalizing differences and inequalities, translates into several explicit references in the budget for 2017.While not being the only target of these policies: inhabitants with a migration background will particularly benefit from these proposals given the gaps in their socio-economic outcomes. Much as including integration in broader social cohesion objectives avoids creating targeted measures, the absence of an integration strategy might reduce public administration capacity for improving coherence among policies that affect migrant population and for identifying obstacles limiting access to universal services and opportunities to migrants and refugees. Building on these 30 proposals, the municipality should continue strengthening its capacity for monitoring disparities in living conditions between different groups and districts. Further the implementation of the 30 proposals should happen through cross-department implementation mechanisms to ensure policy coherence. In this sense the experience of the Migration and integration department in the City of Vienna and the contracts they sign to make sure all relevant departments achieve integration-related objectives could be an example. The intention of equalizing differences and inequalities,

Creating spaces to bring communities together: in addition to new housing projects, the city has set up some public spaces that facilitate equitable access to information about Swedish society and systems available (see the Integration centre and the Cultur house in Angered described in section 2.2) as well as an agenda of multicultural events (see 5.2) and supports grassroots initiatives that provide meeting places for different groups. There is margin to build on these experiences also by drawing from the practices of other cities in creating public spaces that are attractive and affordable for all groups, favouring more social mix (i.e. the centre 104 and Grands Voisins in Paris; the libraries in Barcelona, etc.).

Example of multi-level governance mechanism: the 2010 division of labours for the implementation of *National Introduction Programme* made municipalities responsible for providing housing, language classes, initiatives for children in schools and pre-school as well as civic orientation services while the national level – the Public Employment Service (PES) - is responsible for all introduction activities for newly arrived adults. This programme, which has provided the template for integration systems across many OECD countries (OECD, 2016[4]), aims at getting people into the labour market as quickly as possible through multi-sectoral measures. As a result of centralising some of the tasks, the homogeneity of some measures increased across territories but they may result as less customised to local needs and opportunities. As previously highlighted (OECD, 2016[4]) (Bakbasel, 2012[5]) this multi-level mechanism could be improved by increasing the opportunities for the PES and the municipalities for designing and evaluating jointly the Introduction programme. For instance the two levels could cooperate directly since the assessment of newcomers' capacities (see section 2.4.1). In addition, reinforced national-local cooperation would allow sharing know-how across Swedish provinces and level-out the effectiveness of these measures. In terms of funding the research highlighted that transfers from the central government could better support municipalities by considering welfare funding needs beyond the Integration Programme for those who cannot find a job after two years. Useful examples could be the national-local roundtable organised by the Dutch ministry of Employment to discuss the implementation of anti-discrimination legislation in the labour market.

Local housing capacities for refugees and asylum seekers: the dual accommodation system (see section 2.1.1) based on the choice of asylum seekers and status holders to find their own accommodation, should be closely assessed in terms of protection and concentration effects at the local level. While allowing asylum seekers and refugees to benefit from family and national networks, and contributing to releasing the pressure from the national dispersal systems, the possibility to receive support to find an accommodation autonomously has, in the view of some interviewees, several unintended consequences. For instance it increased the concentration of newcomers in already segregated areas; it exposes them to the risk of living in overcrowded housing conditions and further increased the presence of foreign pupils in the schools operating in exposed areas. Local authorities should weight the impact that the mechanism offering newcomers the possibility to find their own accommodation across sectors (i.e. educations, health) and in terms of equality across districts. On the other hand, the municipality already fund that the funding available for increasing municipal capacities to find adequate housing solutions for newcomers assigned by the national dispersal mechanism are often insufficient.

Local implications of the national dispersal mechanism: The obligatory mechanism for recognised refugee dispersal implemented since January 2017 is designed for matching places characteristics (i.e. labour market needs; etc.) with newcomers' characteristics (i.e. skills, educational attainment, etc.) thus avoiding second movements (see section2.1.3). Its impact at the local level needs to be closely monitored to establish whether the obligatory character of the new model is more successful in reducing the bottlenecks caused by limited housing and in better matching local labour-market needs with newcomers' skills. According to the information collected from the municipality, multi-level mechanisms of information and funding related to this mechanism could be improved and take into account the feedback received from the municipalities. Experience sharing with other countries implementing similar mechanisms (i.e. Netherlands, Norway, etc.) could be beneficial.

Good practices that could be replicated

Gothenburg has significant control over designing and implementing local integration measures thanks to a variety of mechanisms (e.g. co-operative capacities, municipal enterprises, access to credit, etc.).   The city is determined to focus its action on the competences, qualifications and skills that refugee migrants bring to the inhabitants and use them as leverage to stimulate integration. In addition a diversity of financial resources - in 2016 only 34% of the costs of Gothenburg's integration measures were paid by national contributions- helps in designing autonomous practices for integration.

Implementing integration services at the right scale: the municipality has increased its political efforts in terms of intensifying relations with neighbouring municipalities as well as governmental agencies—such as the Employment Agency, occupational education institutions, higher education institutions- and other levels of government -the region- to provide better services for refugees and migrants. One example is the regional partnership for facilitating the validation of qualifications and skills for work and education (See Validation West paragraph 2.4.4) as well as the Gothenburg Regional Association (section 2.1.1.5.), that is a rare example of municipal cooperation for integration management that could be applied to other regions in Sweden and elsewhere.

Evaluation Mechanisms: A report entitled 'Inequality in living conditions and health in Gothenburg' was produced in 2014. This report produces local data on the disparities in living conditions between different groups and districts. While wellbeing indicators are measured per groups of population in other cities partner of this study – i.e. Diversity scorecard of the city of Amsterdam-; few other cities (i.e. Rome) have measured these outcomes at the district level. The municipality of Gothenburg aims at increasing its capacity to monitor the integration outcomes of newcomers (see section 2.3.3). In this sense the Amsterdam experience in assessing cost and benefits of integration measures could be helpful.

Creating long term housing projects fostering inclusion: among its long-term objectives the city aims at "shortening distances, both between places and people. The city will be more compact with new homes, workplaces and meeting-places". The city defines that tenants, how bought land and right for new housing, ensure that a percentage will have low rents. The city, with housing companies, has the political ambition to develop long-term housing projects (such as the 80 000 units new housing Älvstranden project not yet built) that can be attractive and affordable for different groups, creating more heterogeneous living areas in order to break current patterns of segregation (see section 2.4.2).

Joint programming across municipal services: The development of join programmes between police and the city is an example of horizontal cooperation and of how increased policy coherence can help citizens to feel their city is safer. These activities are based on the security issues raised by citizens in individual districts, as well as youth at risk. This cooperation has the function of building trust between residents of exposed areas as well as preventing exclusion, marginalisation and risk behaviours.

Innovative funding mechanisms: An innovative mechanism for managing EU funding at the regional level has been established in West Sweden "Structural Fund Partnership" (SFP), which coordinates with a number of stakeholders including municipalities, on calls for proposals based on specific regional needs or intentions. This mechanism can gather the intentions and needs of different actors at the local level and jointly apply for EU integration funds.

Involvement of civil society: the substantial involvement of civil society, the positive attitudes towards receiving and welcoming refugees is perhaps not unique to Gothenburg, but nevertheless deserves to be accentuated as a foundation for creating platforms for inclusion. Partnership agreements established between the municipality and non-governmental organisations (see section 2.3.2.), as the ones signed for accommodating unaccompanied minors, provide for examples of sustainable modalities of cooperation and structures of agency.

Various health initiatives such as the Refugee child team, the Crisis and Trauma Clinic (see section 2.4.3) increase the likelihood that the new population's health demands, both in terms of treatment and prevention will be met.

Note

[1] Göteborg & Co is the unit within the city working to promote tourism and events. Here, there is cooperation between the private sector and the universities and this platform could be utilised for collaboration aiming towards inclusion.

Key data on migrant presence and integration in Gothenburg

Gothenburg (Swedish: Göteborg)

Figure 1. Gothenburg, Vastra Gotland County

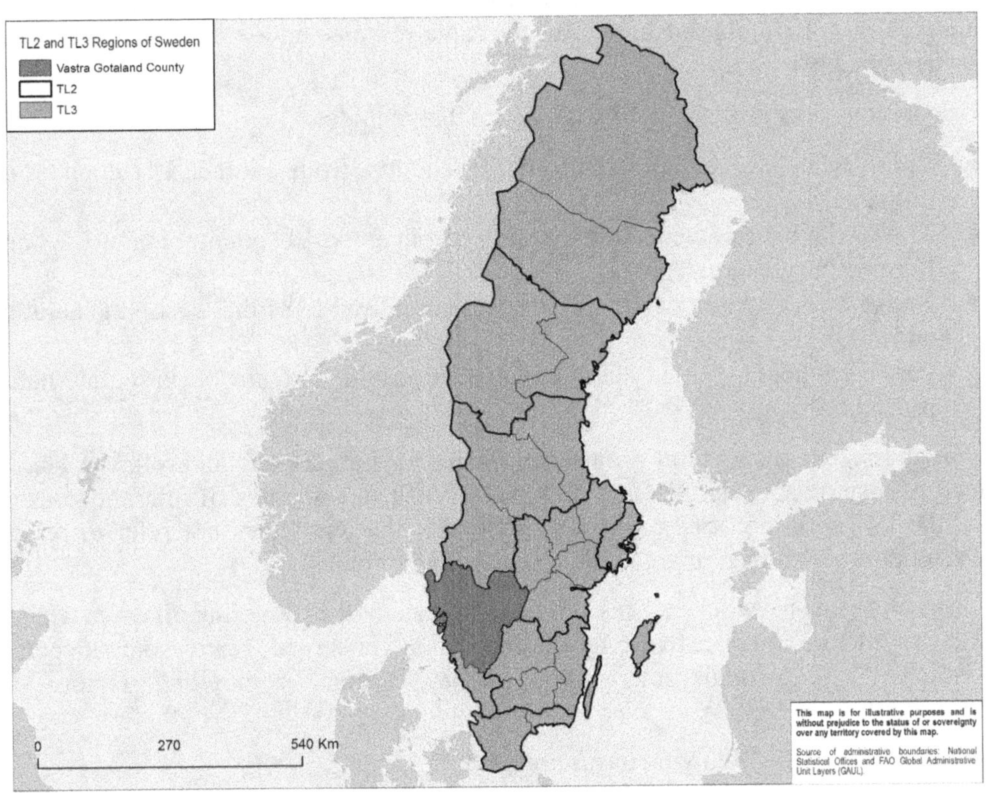

Note: Västra Götaland is composed of 49 municipalities among which Gothenburg. TL2: Territorial Level 2 consists of the OECD classification of regions within each member country. There are 335 regions classified at this level across 35 member countries.TL3: Territorial Level 3 consists of the lower level of classification and is composed of 1 681 small regions. In most cases, they correspond to administrative regions.
Source. OECD (2018), OECD Regional Statistics Database, http://dx.doi.org/10.1787/region-data-en.

Municipality	TL3	TL2	State
Gothenburg	Västra Götaland	Västsverige or West Sweden	Sweden

Definition of migrant

The term 'migrant' generally functions as an umbrella term used to describe people that move to another country with the intention of staying for a significant period of time. According to the United Nations (UN), a long-term migrant is "a person who moves to a country other than that of his or her usual residence for a period of at least a year (12 months)". Yet, not all migrants move for the same reasons, have the same needs or come under the same laws.

This report considers migrants as a large group that includes:

- Those who have emigrated to an EU country from another EU country ('EU migrants'),
- Those who have come to an EU country from a non-EU country ('non-EU born or third-country national'),
- Native-born children of immigrants (often referred to as the 'second generation'), and
- Persons who have fled their country of origin and are seeking international protection.

For the latter, some distinctions are needed. While asylum seekers and refugees are often counted as a subset of migrants and included in official estimates of migrant stocks and flows, the UN definition of 'migrant' is clear that the term does not refer to refugees, displaced, or others forced or compelled to leave their homes:

The term 'migrant' in Article 1.1 (a) should be understood as covering all cases where the decision to migrate is taken freely by the individual concerned, for reasons of 'personal convenience' and without intervention of an external compelling factor. (IOM Constitution Article 1.1 (a)).

Thus, in this report the following terms are used:

- 'Status holder' or 'refugee' for those who have successfully applied for asylum and have been granted some sort of protection in their host country, including those who are recognised as 'refugees' on the basis of the 1951 Geneva Convection Relating to the Status of Refugees, but also those benefiting from national asylum laws or EU legislation (Directive 2011/95/EU), such as the subsidiary protection status.
- 'Asylum seeker' for those who have submitted a claim for international protection but are awaiting the final decision are referred.
- 'Rejected asylum seeker' for those who have been denied protection status.
- 'Undocumented migrants' for those who decide not to appeal the decision on their asylum seeker status or do not apply for another form of legal permission to stay.

This report systematically distinguishes which group is targeted by policies and services put in place by the city. Where statistics provided by the cities included refugees in the migrant stocks and flows, it will be indicated accordingly.

Sources: (UNSD, 2017), IOM Constitution Article 1.1 (a)), EU legislation (Directive 2011/95/EU), (OECD, 2016c).

In contrast to other countries, statistics on the immigrant population in Sweden use the "background" of the population as an important distinction. "Swedish" or "native" background indicates a person who is born in Sweden and whose parents were both born in Sweden. "Foreign background" indicates an individual who was born abroad, or whose parents were born abroad. The statistics in Sweden sometimes allow distinguishing between migrants born abroad and whose parents were born abroad. This last category will be referred to in the case study as second-generation migrants or children of foreign born.

When it comes to migrants, the National Migration Agency, keeps statistics in relation to the reasons for coming to Sweden, i.e. whether for employment, studies, family reunification or seeking asylum. The category of newly-arrived migrants includes all "third country national" migrants who have received their first residency permit within 36 months (European Commission, 2017[6]). Referring to refugees, categories that are employed are: asylum seekers (in itself a category divided into different claimed reasons for seeking asylum) and "newly arrived" or "newcomers" (nyanlända) refugees (i.e. having received a residence permit in the past two or maximum three years). Children in primary school can be newcomers for four years. There is no specific category "vulnerable migrants" although of course, unaccompanied minors remain a specific category of vulnerability, as are "undocumented" as well as "hidden" refugees. Undocumented migrants have no legal permit of residence in Sweden and hidden refugees refer to people whose application for asylum has been rejected, but who have decided to stay without a legal permit.

Key statistics

Gothenburg is the second largest city in Sweden with 556 039 inhabitants (31 December 2017), is part of Gothenburg regional association (997 446 inhabitants). The city is located in the county of Västra Götaland (TL3) with 1 690 782 inhabitants and in the national area of West Sweden (TL2).

The following table contains data for West Sweden (TL2) 2014-2015 and is the result of an ad hoc extraction from the new database developed by the Regional Development Policy Division (CFE) in partnership with the International Migration Division (ELS) of the OECD.

Table 1. Outcomes: Migrant VS Native population in West Sweden (TL2)

West Sweden (TL2)	Foreign born in the region (absolute values)	Foreign born in the region (% values)	Swedish born in the region (absolute values)	Swedish born in the region (% values)	Foreign born in Sweden (absolute values)	Foreign born in Sweden (% values)	Swedish born in Sweden (abs values)	Swedish born in SWE (% values)
A. Presence	357177	18.39	1 585 503	81.61	1 859 267	19.07	7 888 093	80.93
B. Employment	146794	64.94	794 185	79.15	44 5115	52.43	3 646 755	73.6
C. Unemployment	26418	15.25	46 110	5.49	37 580	7.79	10 8945	2.9
D. Overqualification	18667	12.72	41796	5.26	59 779	13.43	17 9249	4.92
E. Primary	72768	32.19	133127	13.27	252395	29.66	1 375 360	25.02
F. Secondary	76421	33.81	513305	51.15	393090	46.2	2 868 930	52.19
G. Tertiary	76865	34	357015	35.58	205450	24.14	1 252 905	22.79
H. Rooms per capita		1.23		1.52		1.22		1.48
I. Immigration good for country's economy (0 to 10)				5.46				5.67
J. Allow immigrants of different race/ethnic group			1401291	88.38			6897889	87.45
K. Dependency ratio		9.32		15.85		9.23		16.2

Note: the following definitions apply to the table above
Source: OECD database on migrant population outcome at TL2 level.

Definition	Absolute values	Relative values
A. Presence	Total	Share on total population (0+ years old)
B. Employment	Total	Employment rate (%): share of employed on total working-age population (15-64 years old)
C. Unemployment	Total	Unemployment rate (%): share of unemployed on total labour force (15-64 years old)
D. Overqualification	Total of those with "high" level of education and in low or medium skilled jobs	Overqualification rate (%): share of overqualified workers on total employed (15-64 years old)
E. Primary	Total with primary education	Share on total working age population (%) (ages 15-64 and excluding those currently in education or training)
F. Secondary	Total with secondary education	

G. Tertiary	Total with tertiary education	
H. Rooms per capita		Average number or rooms per inhabitant
I. Immigration good for country's economy (0 to 10)		Average value on the scale 0 to 10, where 10 is the most positive opinion
J. Allow immigrants of different race/ethnic group	Total	Share on total population of people that believe immigrants should be allow into the country (%)
K. Dependency ratio		Share of dependent population (0-14 & 65+ years old) on total population (0+ years old) (%)

Statistics for the City of Gothenburg and national level

The figures below are extracted from questionnaire the developed by OECD filled by the city of Gothenburg in February 2017, from Swedish Central Bureau of Statistics (SCB), from the National Migration Agency and the from Municipality of Gothenburg (Göteborgs stads stadsledningskontor: Samhällsanalys och statistic). Also other reports, studies and research material have been utilised for a more complete picture, please see the reference list.

1. Presence of population

1.1 Country Population: 9.696 million inhabitants (2014)

Number of counties 21 with 290 municipalities

Sub-national governments are responsible for 47.4% of public expenditure – OECD average = 40%, Sweden is the 5th most decentralised country in the OECD

Share of sub-central government revenues in total revenues: 79.5%

Share of taxes in sub-central government revenues: 53.7%

City composition - # of districts: 10 districts

1.2 Total city population

556 039 (31 December 2017); *4,400 new residents in 2016*

34% of the population has a foreign background (31 December 2016); as mentioned above, in Swedish statistics ''Foreign background'' indicates an individual who was born abroad, or whose parents were born abroad. Foreign background can be nationals (having Swedish nationality).

146 937 persons were born abroad or 26% of the population (31 December 2017)

62 513 persons had foreign citizenship or 11% of the population (31 December 2017)

As comparison, in Sweden in 2016 18%% of the total population of Sweden was born outside of the country (SCB statistics 2017). In 2015, this stood at 16%% of the population and half of the foreign-born arrived to Sweden as refugees (OECD, 2016[7]).

1.3 In terms of length of stay

In Gothenburg the majority of migrants are first generation who arrived more than 10 years ago (41.7%) followed by second generation migrants who represent 26.1%, recent migrants represent only 4.4% whereas the rest remained up to 5 years (13.5%) or between 5 and 10 years (13%). Almost half of the migrant population is in the age cohort 53-65 (48.3%) and the second biggest cohort is composed of migrants between 25 and 35 years of age (23.2%).

1.4 Migrants' most important countries of origin in Gothenburg:

(December 2017) 5 Most common citizenship countries: Syria (8%), Somalia (7%), Poland (5%), India (5%) and Finland (5%).

(December 2017) 5 most common birth countries: Iraq (9%), Iran (8%), Somalia (6%), Bosnia and Hercegovina (5%), Syria (5%).

1.5 Number of Asylum seekers and recognised refugees - National figures

In 2015, 162 877 asylum seekers arrived in Sweden in total; 35 369 of them were unaccompanied minors.

In 2016, the total number of asylum seekers were 28 939; 2 199 of them were unaccompanied minors.

Reasons for permits of residence:

2016 residence permits 105 530, divided into: 24 000 labour market migration, 39 000 relatives, 72 000 asylum seekers and refugees; 4 300 EU/EES; 11 000 students. (OECD, 2017[8])

It is estimated that in the autumn of 2016 there were 4 000 EU-migrants in Sweden, a decline since 2015 (http://www.sydsvenskan.se/2016-10-01/farre-eu-migranter-i-sverige-infor-vintern).

''Undocumented migrants'' there are no adequate numbers, but estimations from 2010 claim that there were at that time between 10 000 and 35 000 undocumented migrants in Sweden (Migrationsinfo 2016). That figure has likely increased substantially since 2010.

"Hidden refugees" from the presentation of the Migration Agency to the OECD delegation (Gothenburg, March 15th 2017) the number of asylum seekers whose application has been rejected but who continue to live in the country was around 5 800 in Sweden in 2016.

1.6 Number of asylum seekers and recognised refugees – Gothenburg figures

In February 2017, there were 4 704 asylum seekers living in accommodation provided for by the Migration Agency, in Gothenburg as compared to 4 548 persons in December 2016 and 6 193 in 2015.

In 2016, 3 321 persons took up residence in Gothenburg after the asylum seeking process and approval of residence permit; 445 of those were unaccompanied minors

In the period 2010–2016; a total number of 12 858 took up residence in Gothenburg after approval of residence permits, 1 003 of whom were unaccompanied minors

The most important countries of origin for asylum seekers in 2016: Syria, Iraq, Afghanistan, Eritrea, Somalia, stateless.

2. Employment

2.1 Employment rate including part-time employed

For Gothenburg as a whole, 76.1% were employed in 2014. 84.3% of those with a Swedish background were employed, compared to 61.2% of those with a foreign background

2.2 Full time unemployed

% for migrant population; % for national

6.2% of the population of Gothenburg was unemployed in 2014; 3.6% of those with a Swedish background and 12.6% of those with a foreign background.

2.3 Population at risk of poverty

% for migrant population; % for national

National figure: In 2014, 15% of the population in Sweden faced the risk of poverty, 12% of Swedish-born and 34% of those born outside of the EU

2.4 Overqualification rate:

Difference in labour market participation rate between non migrant VS migrant background when the person holds a post-secondary or university degree

National figures: In 2014, 11% of foreign born were employed in jobs that required a little education but had a long postsecondary education; the corresponding figure for Swedish born was 3%

2.5 Share of self-employment

% for migrant population; % for national

The proportion of self-employed in Sweden is higher among those who have a foreign background than those with a Swedish background. The most common sector for foreign born self-employed is restaurants and hotels, whereas for the Swedish born, the construction sector is larger. For instance in 2012, 4.8% of Swedish born men were self-employed; 7.7% of men born in Iran; 11.4% of men born in Syria, and 1.0% of men born in Somalia (Aldén & Hammarstedt, 2017).

3. Right to vote

Right of resident eligible for voting who are excluded from this right because of foreign citizenship.

The right to vote in the parliamentary elections is for Swedish citizens who reside in Sweden or who have at some time lived in Sweden and who are at least 18 years of age. The right to vote in municipal and regional elections also includes foreign citizens who have been registered in Sweden for three years or more. Citizens of EU-member states, Norway and Iceland have the right to vote in those elections if they have been registered for 30 days and have notified a wish to vote.

In the parliamentary elections 2014, 12% of those entitled to vote were born outside Sweden. The voter turnout was 89%%among those born in Sweden, compared to 72% among those who were foreign born. The turnout is in general lower among the part of the population that was born in Asia, Africa or Europe outside of EU. It also tends to be lower among those individuals who have lived in Sweden for a shorter period of time.

In the municipal election in Gothenburg in 2010, 54% of the population that was entitled to vote actually did vote in Norra Angered, the corresponding figure for the Southwest areas was 89%.

4. Educational Attainment (Primary; Secondary; University)

% for migrant population; % for national

In 2015, 10% of the Swedish-background population in Gothenburg had only primary education, versus 21% of those with a foreign background; 37% of Swedish-background and 36% of those with a foreign background had secondary education; 19% of Swedish background and 14% of those with a foreign background had a post-secondary education shorter than three years, and 33% of Swedish background and 23% of those with a foreign background had a post-secondary education of three years or more; for 0.4% of Swedish background and 6% of those with a foreign background, the level of education was unknown.

5. Net annual migrant household income

The middle income for Gothenburg in total was SEK 269 503 in 2014; SEK 302 056 for those with a Swedish background and SEK 200 926 for those with a foreign background, or 74% of the middle income for the total population.

National 2017 GDP per capita (USD at PPP): USD 46 419 = SEK 376 251

(OECD, 2017[9])

6. Main industrial sectors

Where migrants work: Construction, human health and social work services, whole and retail trade; repair of motor vehicles, transportation and storage, hotel and restaurants and food service activities as well as in the education sector.

Introduction

The objective of this case study is to provide an analysis of refugee and migrant reception and integration policies and related multilevel governance mechanisms in Gothenburg. It should be noted that most of the immigration to Sweden in recent decades has involved refugees, which is thus the focus of this study.

It is not within the scope or ambition of this report, to represent an exhaustive analysis of issues related to the integration of migrants in Gothenburg which will require a thorough analysis of each area related to integration.

This report takes as a starting point a multi-dimensional definition of integration:

The effective integration of migrants is not an economic and labour-market process alone. It also has social, educational – even spatial – facets. None, though, are mutually exclusive: disadvantage and the failure to integrate in one dimension are likely to have multiple repercussions. Concentrations of migrants in geographically disadvantaged areas, for example, may affect effective integration in the education system and, later, the labour market (OECD 2015).

There is often a risk in conceptualising integration as making migrants ''fit'' into host societies; from the point of view of host states' structures and needs, rather than from the perspective of refugees and migrants (Eastmond 2011; Olwig 2011). The objective of this case study is to emphasize the multi-dimensionality of integration processes and the need to consider the different points of view of the actors involved. Newcomers settling in a new society can enhance its potential for resilience, innovation and well-being. Through empowerment and its various agencies and services the city can shape this opportunity.

This report takes stock of the multilevel institutional and legal framework within which such actions are implemented and identifies best practices that could be implemented elsewhere as well as the bottlenecks where the city struggles. This work builds on previous OECD recommendations with regard to migrant integration in Sweden that already observed that "thanks to their awareness of local realities and their proximity to citizens and businesses, subnational governments are well placed to promote a cohesive policy approach to the integration of migrants across policy domains such as education, employment, housing, health and culture, working closely with the central government through effective multilevel governance. The central government should be working with local governments to identify best practices at the local level and disseminate good practice to other areas in Sweden that might be struggling with the integration of migrants" (OECD/UCLG, 2016[10]).

Box 1. Source of information for the Case Study

The report is based on the following material and extraction of information:

- An extensive questionnaire designed by the OECD and completed by representatives of the City of Gothenburg in the beginning of 2017. Some statistics have been updated in March 2018;
- Statistics from the Swedish Central Bureau of Statistics (SCB), the National Migration Agency and the Municipality of Gothenburg (Göteborgs stads stadsledningskontor: Samhällsanalys och statistik). It is important to note that the statistics used by the municipality are often based on the district level. In a larger report on varying living conditions throughout the city, published in 2014, statistics are broken down to smaller units (Göteborgs stad 2014). Sometimes, those figures are used in the report.
- Reports and studies by official authorities, OECD and private institutions;
- Research reports and papers conducted by scholars, mostly from the University of Gothenburg, but also from other universities;
- Media sources: Interviews conducted during the OECD field mission 15-17 March 2017 with representatives from the Gothenburg municipality as well as other stakeholders representing national government authorities, regional actors, the private sector as well as civil society and migrants. A full list is presented as an appendix to this report.

The study is structured in two parts. **Part One** offers a snapshot of migration in Gothenburg today, including stock, historic migrant and refugee flows and nationalities, key laws, and the main issues emerging in the city related to migrant integration. **Part Two** presents the national context within which the city acts and the city's institutions relevant to integration and the responses for reception and integration of migrants and refugees. These responses are presented according to the objectives identified in the OECD's "Checklist for public action to migrant integration at the local level" (OECD, 2018[1]). The first block of the Checklist presents the multi-level governance setting that applies to Gothenburg's integration policy; the institutional mapping helps to clarify the allocation of competences across levels of government. The second block describes how integration solutions are designed over a period of time and aim to create close collaboration among all groups. The third block overviews operational, capacity building and monitoring tools used by the city for policy implementation. The last block introduces sectoral actions to facilitate integration through labour market, education, housing and social services.

Part I. Migration snapshot: National level and in the city of Gothenburg

Chapter 1. Migration insights: Flows, stock and nationality

Migration flows and approach

Sweden has a longstanding history of migration. People have migrated to Sweden since the 1500s. Gothenburg has a history as a city of commerce, trade, shipyard and manufacturing. The Swedish East India Company was settled in Gothenburg in the 18th century. It has been characterised by immigration since the 1600s, with Dutch architecture helping construct the canal system and the British contributing to trade and industrialisation of the city during the 1700s and 1800s.

During almost a century (between the 1850s to the 1930s), Sweden was a country of large-scale emigration as poor peasants and workers made the hazardous journey across the Atlantic for economic as well as political reasons and in order to try to find better living conditions. Between 1860 and 1930 approximately 1.4 million individuals left Sweden (OECD, 2016b[2]). Gothenburg was, during the time of the great emigration, the main port of departure.

Since World War II, Sweden has been a country of immigration (see Strömbäck 2016). Refugees (many from the Baltic states) and war survivors arrived in the aftermath of World War II. In parallel, from the 1950s and until the early 1970s, there was a fairly large inflow of labour migrants, in particular from Finland, Greece, Italy, Turkey and the former Yugoslavia. In Gothenburg, many worked in car production (Volvo), but also in bearings manufacturing (SKF) and in the leading shipyard industry. For more details on history of migration in Sweden please see (OECD, 2016[11]).

In relation to the oil crisis in 1973 and the shipping crisis, labour migration declined, and since then, Sweden's immigration policies have largely focused on refugees and family reunification. Labour migration has picked up since 2008 but has remained relatively stable and between 2004 and 2013 over 20% of permanent migrant inflows to Sweden were made up of people seeking international protection, and another 40% arrived to reunite with family members (OECD, 2016[11]). The leading refugee groups were Vietnamese, following the Vietnam war, Latin Americans during the 1970s and 1980s, Middle Eastern minority groups (Assyrians, Kurds) during the 1980s, fleeing the Iran-Iraq war or the 1979Iranian revolution, from the horn of Africa, Palestinians from Lebanon, Bosnians and Croats during the Yugoslav war as well as Iraqis between 2003 and 2011.

The aim of Swedish integration policy can be summarised as 'promoting equal rights, obligations and opportunities for all, regardless of ethnic or cultural background which should be reached through general measures for the whole population' (Regerungskansliet, 2009[12]). Despite this 'universal approach', integration measures started as early as 1970 when free language training was introduced for all immigrants and since then the rights of immigrants have been systematically extended and immigrants (mainly refugees and family members) have received targeted support in their first years in Sweden (Bakbasel, 2012[5]). Sweden has a long tradition in providing a home for many migrants fleeing war and persecution. Integration politics, other than language training, rarely target labour migrants and are most often oriented towards refugees. Of course, labour migrants benefit from health, social and school services – just like any other Swede – but are not targeted by specific labour integration policies as most of them are already employed (see section 2.4.3).

Today: Stock and migration law

Sweden is meeting demographic challenges with an elderly population, and low levels of reproduction. An increase in the population through immigration is, according to most economic analysts, seen as positive for long-term development and growth. Some reports indicate that growth is related to the influx of refugees, as it creates new jobs and increases consumption (Scocco & Andersson, 2015).

Today, non-Swedish inhabitants in Sweden represent 19% of the total population (2014-2015 data extraction from OECD Database on regional migration outcomes) and largely originate from Finland (10%), Iraq (8%), Poland (5%), Iranian, Syrian (4%) and Somali (4%) (OECD, 2016[11]). Some 4 000 EU migrants were estimated to be living in Sweden in autumn 2016, Roma from Romania and Bulgaria have been arriving in Sweden for a number of years (Swedish Migration Agency).

Gothenburg is the second largest city of Sweden and has a population of 556 640 (2016). Immigrants account for 25% of the population and 34% of the general population has a foreign background (Göteborgs stad 2016). The city is situated along the coast in the region of Västra Götaland, one of Sweden's 21 geographical and administrative regions and one of the two counties (Västra Götaland and Halland) that form the Västsverige region, which itself is one of the eight Riksomraden regions in Sweden. In comparison in the Västsverige region, foreign-born represent 18.4% of the population (2014-2015 data extraction from OECD Database on regional migration outcomes) and foreign workers accounted for 14% of the regional labour force in 2009. In Gothenburg in 2009 the most of the non-nationals, nearly a quarter of them, came from Scandinavia and about two thirds of all non-nationals came from third countries with the largest group being from Iraq (9%) (Bakbasel, 2012[5]).

The main legal framework regulating immigration to Sweden is the Law on Foreigners (*Utlänningslagen* 2005: 716). A person is automatically Swedish if at least one parent is a Swedish citizen. In order to receive a work permit, one needs to have been offered a job beforehand, and to have applied for the permit before arriving in Sweden (Arbetsformedlingen, 2016[13]). Work permit applications are usually filed from outside Sweden; it is not possible to apply for a work permit and search for a job in Sweden except for people who are studying in the country, which represented 3% of work permits issued in 2016 (OECD, 2017[8]). When it comes to labour migration, 12 526 permits for work were granted in 2016 as compared to 16 900 in 2015 (Migration Agency 2016, Statistics: Work Permits granted). Most of them were in the IT sector (e.g. IT architects or developers), but many also work as civil engineers or engineers. Most jobs in this category required post-secondary education. Another significant sector for persons seeking a work permit to come to Sweden is, however, low-paid and agricultural or forestry work, such as blueberry picking.

Recent asylum seekers and refugee arrivals and legislation

Since 2012, there has been an increase in the number of asylum seekers and in 2015, Sweden experienced the largest intake of asylum seekers in modern times. In that year, there were 162 877 applications for asylum representing 12.3% of the EU total (Swedish

Migration Agency statistics). Over 70 000 were children and 35 000 of them were unaccompanied minors. Most asylum seekers were from Syria, Afghanistan, Iraq, Somalia, Eritrea and there is also the 'stateless' category[1]. In 2016 and 2017, Turkey and Georgia appeared as new countries-of-origin (ibid). However in 2016, the total number of asylum applications in Sweden was 29 000 (Migration Agency statistics), the lowest number since 2010.

The increased arrivals raised questions among Swedish public opinion with regards to the capacity of Swedish welfare institutions to receive and in the longer term integrate large numbers of refugees. A change in asylum legislation was introduced in 2016, including greater scrutiny of reasons for asylum and temporary residence permits, as well as border controls resulting in a decrease in the numbers of asylum seekers. Since 1 January 2017, the Migration Agency is responsible for assigning status holders who need assistance in arranging accommodation to municipalities across the country (see figure 3.1 below). The distribution is based on a combination of criteria including size of the municipality, labour opportunities and capacity to receive (for a more detailed analysis please see section 4.3.1). With the large influx of refugees in 2014 and 2015, the Migration Agency has had difficulties in managing all applications for asylum and the time to process them has been protracted. In 2016, the average time that was required to handle an application was 328 days (Migration agency statistics 2016) compared to 125 days in 2013. With fewer applications, it is expected that the process will be more rapid, reducing the time asylum seekers have to live in the uncertainty of being sent back.

Figure 1.1. Asylum seekers per steps of the application process in 2016 in Sweden

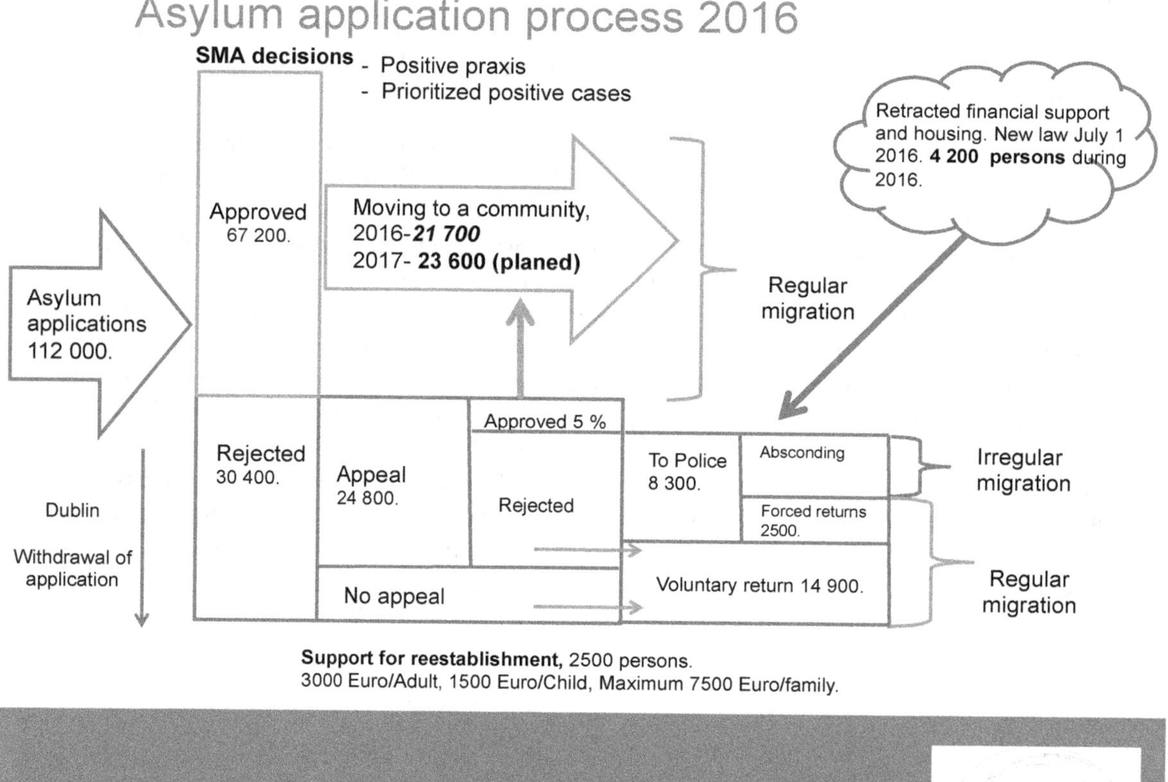

Source: Swedish Migration Agency, March 2017.

The Vastra Gotaland Ian region hosts the highest absolute number of asylum seekers of all Swedish regions (see figure 3.2 below) however in relative terms they represent only 1% of the population and places Vastra Gotaland Ian among the regions receiving fewer asylum seekers in relative terms (Figure 1.1).

Figure 1.2. Presence of asylum seekers in the accommodation system per region at TL3 level in Sweden in 2017 –absolute figures

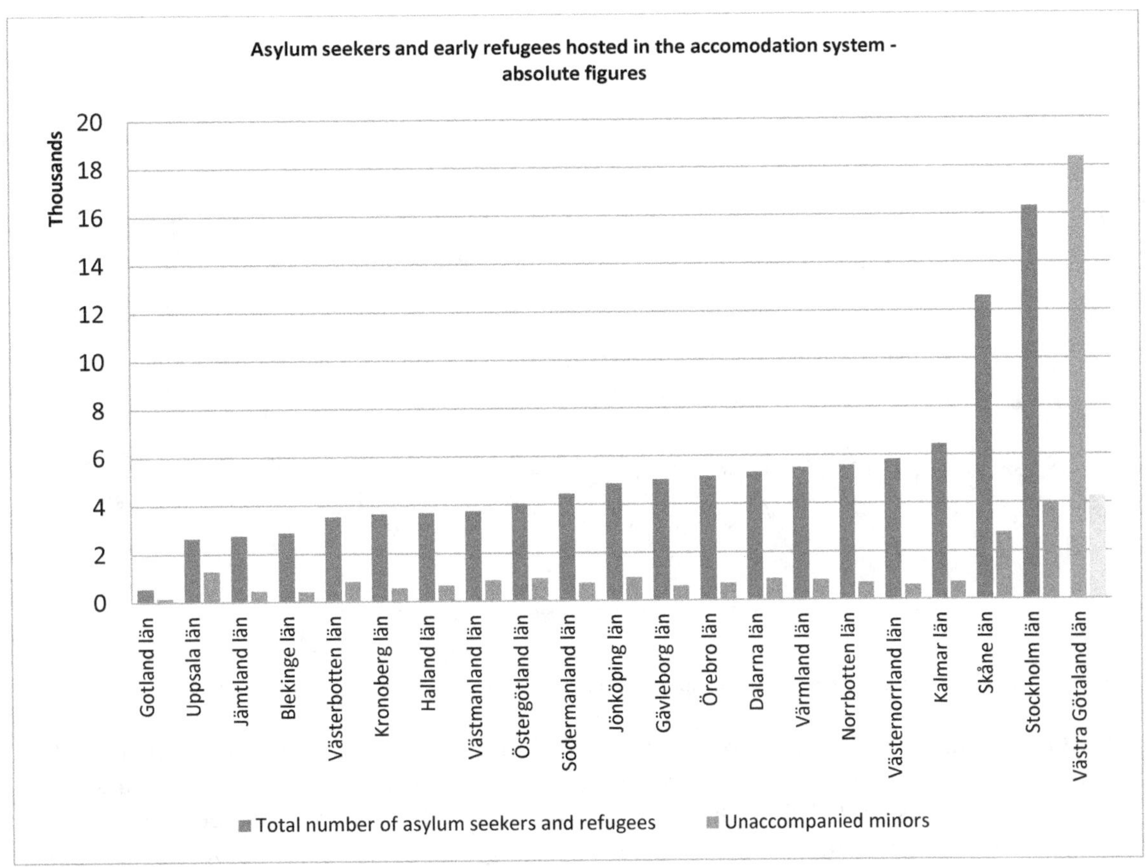

Source. OECD database on presence of asylum seekers distribution at TL3 level, forthcoming.

Figure 1.3. Presence of asylum seekers in the accommodation system per region at TL3 level in Sweden in 2017 – relative figures

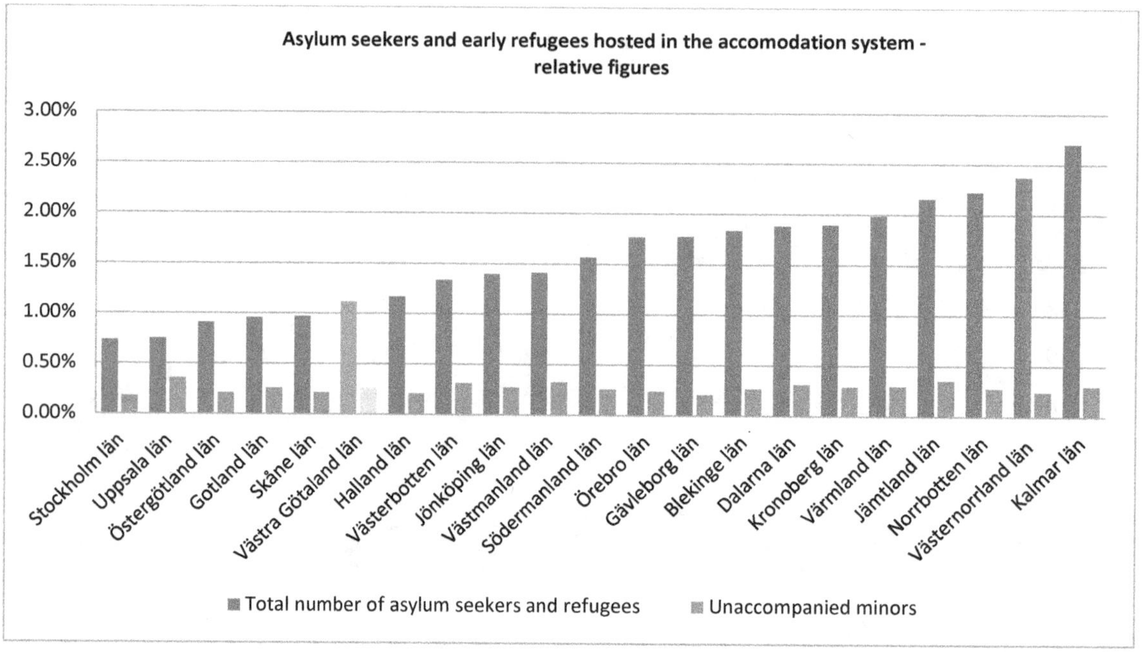

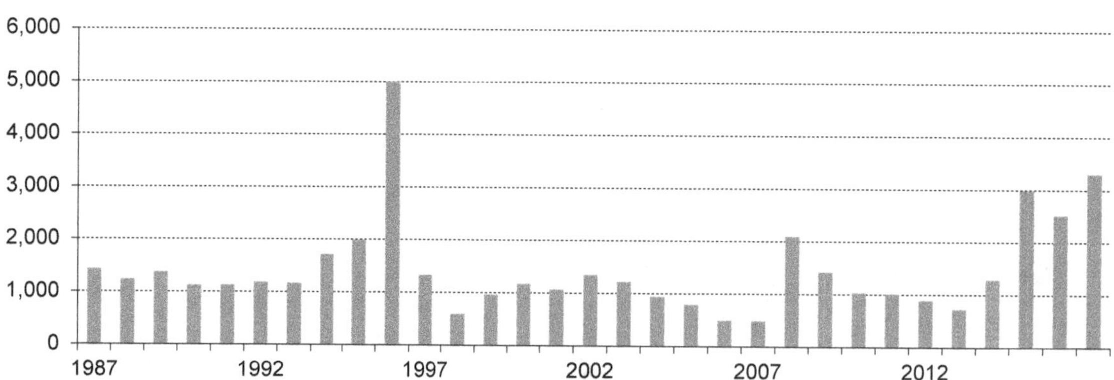

Source. OECD database on presence of asylum seekers distribution at TL3 level, forthcoming

In Gothenburg in 2016, there were 3 321 recognised refugees of which 455 unaccompanied minors and 4 704 asylum seekers (in January 2017), which was a steep decrease compared to 6 193 asylum seekers hosted in 2015. As we can see from figure 3.4 below, another peak of refugees in Gothenburg was reached in 1996, when 5 000 refugees arrived mainly from Iraq and the Balkans.

Figure 1.4. Number of refugees per year in Gothenburg 1987-2016

Source: Social resource management Gothenburg 2016

City well-being and inclusion

Figure 1.5. Well-being in West Sweden 2017

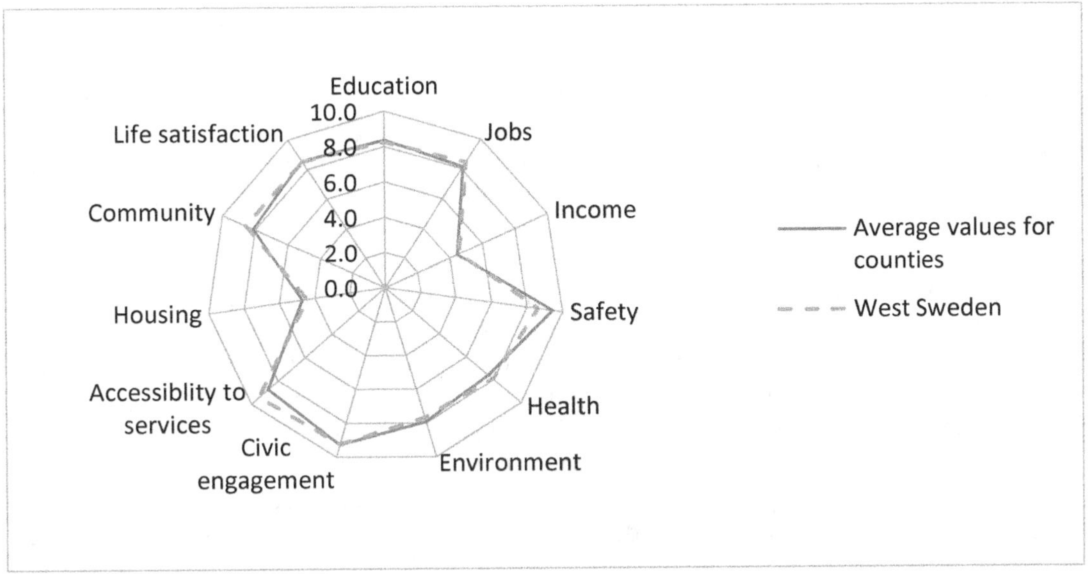

Source: ad-hoc analysis based on OECD well-being dataset on Västsverige-West Sweden region (2017).

Well-being in the region of West Sweden (Västsverige region), where Gothenburg is located, is very similar to the national average. However, the region is performing slightly worse in the following dimensions: housing, environment, safety and education, equally in life satisfaction and civic engagement and slightly better in accessibility of services, health, jobs, income and sense of community (ad-hoc analysis based on OECD well-being dataset 2017).

Historically, Gothenburg has been a city of trade, commerce, shipyards and industry. Being the largest port in Scandinavia and one of the largest in Northern Europe, the city is home to one third of Sweden's exports and imports (Business Region Göteborg 2016). Important industrial companies originating in Gothenburg include Volvo and SKF.

The Gothenburg region represents today a growing economy. One of the fastest growing industrial branches is the medical industry. The global pharmaceutical company AstraZeneca is based in Gothenburg where the bulk of research activities are located, which provides for close collaboration between the company and the universities situated in the city (Chalmers and the University of Gothenburg). Tourism and the IT-sector are also examples of sectors representing rapid growth. More than 100 000 new jobs have been created since 2000, and the pace of growth is expected to accelerate further with several new development projects, including city planning of building and expansion (Business Region Göteborg 2016).

The two universities in the city further contribute to the city's profile as knowledge intensive and also providing for close collaboration between research, policy, innovation and entrepreneurship.

Large disparities and inequalities between different parts and districts make Gothenburg a segregated city. In general, Sweden has a high rate of residential segregation by ethnicity when compared internationally (Andersson, 2010[14]). Although Sweden is still one of the most egalitarian countries in the OECD, the increase in inequalities in living conditions between 1985 and the late 2000s is the most rapid among all OECD countries (OECD 2015). Urban geographical segregation in Sweden has its roots in the so-called ''million programme'' (*miljonprogrammet*), established during the late 1960s and early 1970s. The goal was to come to terms with housing shortages through building one million residences, mostly rental apartments in tall buildings outside of the city centre. Suburbs were created and mostly inhabited, at first, by the working class. Between 1970 and 1990, many of these original residents moved out, leaving empty apartments and residential towers behind. Those who stayed were generally people in relatively difficult social situations. Since the 1990s, many refugees have moved into these areas. As the number of asylum seekers increased in 2014 and 2015, this pattern was reinforced in some Swedish cities. Some of these areas are called by Swedish public authorities "exposed areas'' and are frequently associated with high unemployment, low income, lower levels of education and health, poor results in school and a sometimes marginal youths. The police have identified 15 areas/neighbourhoods in Sweden as particularly ''exposed''; six of these are within Gothenburg (Polisen 2015). There has, over time, been targeted action plans to address inequalities across specific areas (Thörnquist: 22) and the city is committed to measuring disparities across its neighbourhoods. To this end, it produces the 'Göteborgsbladet'[2], which is an annual report providing key statistics for each subdivision of the city. Most of the data used in the following paragraphs are extracted from that report.

Figure 1.6. Gothenburg and its districts 2016

Source: Google Maps.

Figure 1.7. Percentage (%) of persons foreign born by sub-district

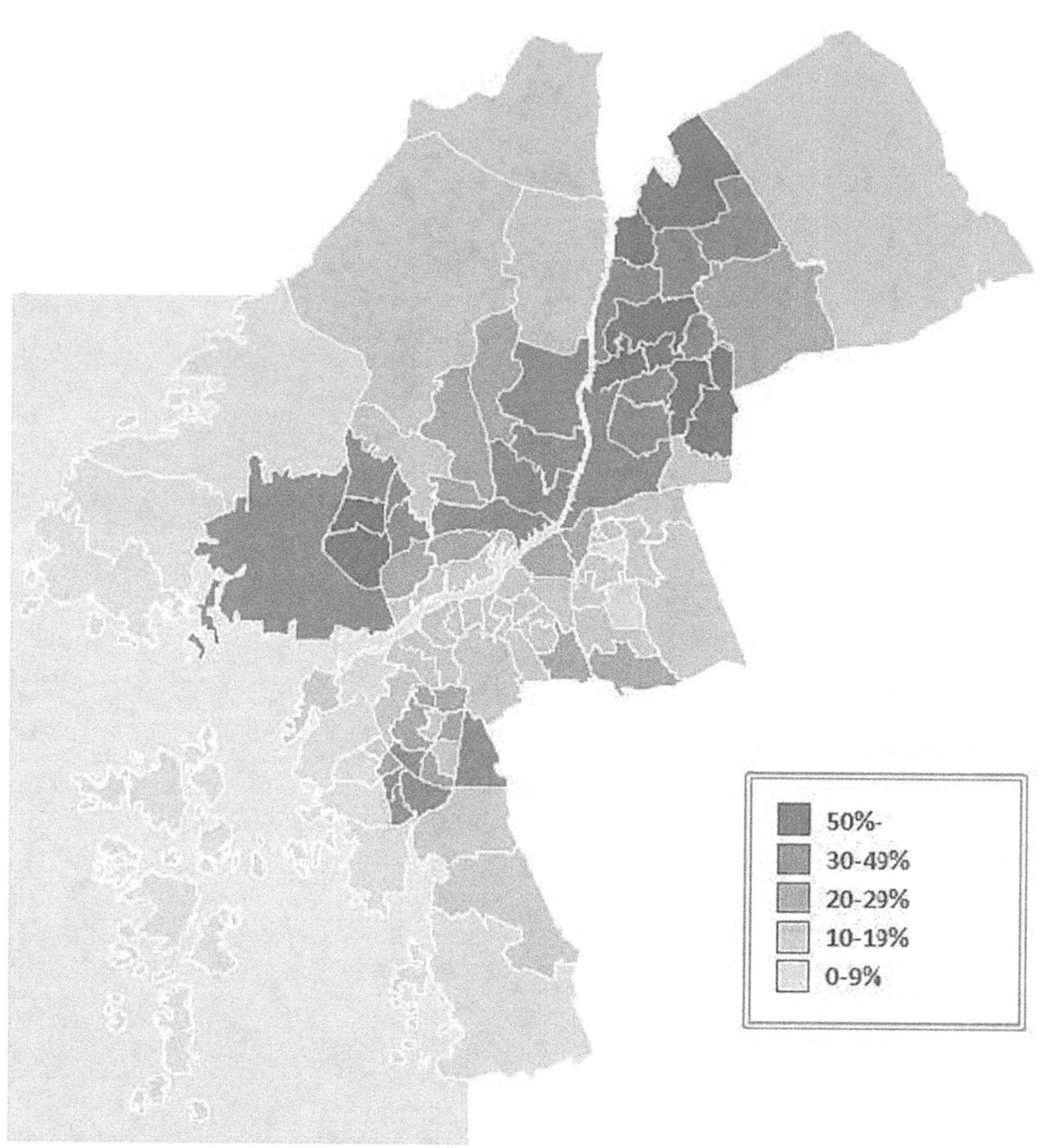

Note: The average % of foreign born in Gothenburg is 26%.
Source: Göteborgs stad, Stadsledningskontoret Statistik och analys. December 2017.

Table 1.1. Percentage of population with a foreign background and foreign born in the districts and Gothenburg as a whole

District	Percentage of foreign background	Percentage foreign born	District	Percentage of foreign background
Angered(Gunnared and Lärjedalen)	73.4	51.0	Angered(Gunnared and Lärjedalen)	73.4
Östra Göteborg (Bergsjön and Kortedala)	57.0	42.4	Östra Göteborg (Bergsjön and Kortedala)	57.0
Örgryte/Härlanda	19.0	14.7	Örgryte/Härlanda	19.0
Centrum	22.7	18.0	Centrum	22.7
Majorna/Linné	18.4	14.5	Majorna/Linné	18.4
Askim/Frölunda/Högsbo	23.7	18.1	Askim/Frölunda/Högsbo	23.7
Västra Göteborg (Långedrag)	22.1	15.8	Västra Göteborg (Långedrag)	22.1
Västra Hisingen (Torslanda)	37.5	27.9	Västra Hisingen (Torslanda)	37.5
Lundby	30.5	22.7	Lundby	30.5
Norra Hisingen	36.7	25.8	Norra Hisingen	36.7
Gothenburg as a whole	33.1	24.5	Gothenburg as a whole	33.1

Source: Göteborgsbladet 2016

Gothenburg is composed of ten districts (Figure 3.6). Socio-spatial division characterises some of the districts, for instance ''Swedes'' dominate in the Southwest, which is close to the sea, whereas other areas (e.g. the Northeast) are dominated by immigrants (see Figure 3.7 and Table 3.1). Within the same district there can be large differences in terms of origin and well-being. For instance, the district Askim-Frölunda-Högsbo is a microcosm of the segregation in Gothenburg: around the Frölunda torg and in Tynnered neighbourhoods there are still remnants of the million programme, whereas in Fiskebäck and Näset, the population has a high income and live in residential areas with single-family houses. Residential segregation didn't happen overnight, between 1994 and 2005 the number of foreign-born residents increased in nearly every district but more significantly in those districts that already had a high number of foreign-born residents in 1994, showing that the presence of immigrants in an area represented a pull factor for newcomers (Bakbasel, 2012[5]).

Some neighbourhoods are denser in ethnic minorities and are also marked by low socio-economic outcomes in terms of income, education, life expectancy, trust, health, etc. For instance, in Bergsjön (Ostra Gotenburg), 54% of the adult population define themselves as socially isolated, meaning that they consider that they lack friends and social relations, compared to 4% in the South West Coast (Gothenburg, 2014[3]): 106). In North Angered, 51% of the population expresses low trust in other people, compared to 11% in the South West Coast. There are large variations in income throughout the city (Table 3.2). The middle income for Gothenburg in total was SEK 279 000 in 2015; 313 000 for those with a Swedish background and 212 000 for those with a foreign background. In 2010, a person with a foreign background in Gothenburg earned, on average, 64% of the middle income for a person with a Swedish background; in 2015, the gap had decreased to 68% (Göteborgs stad, 2016, statistics).

Table 1.2. Middle income in the districts and Gothenburg as a whole

District	Middle income in SEK
Angered (Gunnared and Lärjedalen)	190 000
Östra Göteborg (Bergsjön and Kortedala)	197 700
Örgryte/Härlanda	297 900
Centrum	291 800
Majorna/Linné	290 300
Askim/Frölunda/Högsbo	300 000
Västra Göteborg	339 300
Västra Hisingen	280 700
Lundby	276 800
Norra Hisingen	266 600
Göteborg as a whole	275 800

Source: Göteborgsbladet 2016

The average income has increased significantly in Gothenburg since 1992; however, it has actually decreased in those districts where it was lowest from the outset (Gothenburg, 2014[3]).

Disparities in living conditions between children with different backgrounds have worsened considerably during the period between 1990 and 2012 (Gothenburg, 2014[3]). In 2013, in the district of Torslanda, 1.5% of children lived in households that could be characterised as poor by the standards used by Save the Children[3], whereas the corresponding figure for Bergsjön was 56% (Göteborgs stad 2014: 64).

Life expectancy varies by 9.1 years for men and 6 years for women between the districts of Bergsjön (73 % foreign background) and Långedrag (22% foreign background population) (Göteborgs stad 2014: 121).

Others variations across districts in terms of access to jobs and education will be described in sections 7.1 and 7.4.

Notes

[1] Most persons in this category are of Palestinian origin.

[2] http://statistik.goteborg.se/Statistik/Faktablad/Goteborgsbladet/Goteborgsbladet-2017/

[3] This definition includes children living in families whose income is not enough to cover basic costs, or families that receive welfare.

Part II. Objectives for effectively integrating migrants and refugees at the local level

This section is structured following the Checklist for public action to migrant integration at the local level, as included in the Synthesis Report (OECD, 2018 Forthcoming [2]) which comprises a list of 12 key evidence-based objectives, that can be used by policy makers and practitioners in the development and implementation of migrant integration programmes, at local, regional, national and international levels. This Checklist highlights for the first time common messages and cross-cutting lessons learnt around policy frameworks, institutions, and mechanisms that feature in policies for migrant and refugee integration.

This innovative tool has been elaborated by the OECD as part of the larger study on "Working Together for Local Integration of Migrants and Refugees" supported by the European Commission, Directorate General for regional and urban policies. The Checklist is articulated according to four blocks and 12 objectives. Part 2 gives a description of the actions implemented in Gothenburg following this framework.

A checklist for public action to migrant integration at the local level

Block 1. Multi-level governance: Institutional and financial settings

Objective 1. Enhance effectiveness of migrant integration policy through improved vertical co-ordination and implementation at the relevant scale.

Objective 2. Seek policy coherence in addressing the multi-dimensional needs of, and opportunities for, migrants at the local level.

Objective 3. Ensure access to, and effective use of, financial resources that are adapted to local responsibilities for migrant integration.

Block 2. Time and space: Keys for migrants and host communities to live together

Objective 4. Design integration policies that take time into account throughout migrants' lifetimes and evolution of residency status.

Objective 5. Create spaces where the interaction brings migrant and native-born communities closer

Block 3. Local capacity for policy formulation and implementation

Objective 6. Build capacity and diversity in civil service, with a view to ensure access to mainstream services for migrants and newcomers

Objective 7. Strengthen co-operation with non-state stakeholders, including through transparent and effective contracts.

Objective 8. Intensify the assessment of integration results for migrants and host communities and their use for evidence-based policies.

Block 4. Sectoral policies related to integration

Objective 9. Match migrant skills with economic and job opportunities.

Objective 10. Secure access to adequate housing.

Objective 11. Provide social welfare measures that are aligned with migrant inclusion.

Objective 12. Establish education responses to address segregation and provide equitable paths to professional growth.

Chapter 2. Block 1. Multi-level governance: Institutional and financial settings

Objective 1.Enhance effectiveness of migrant integration policy through improved vertical co-ordination and implementation at the relevant scale

National level: competences for migration-related matters

In Sweden, migration and integration policies are designed at the national level; however, there is no "integration code" or guidelines that all levels of government have to follow in their integration process. Since the dismantling in 2007of the former Integration Agency – created in 1998 – each ministry and government agency is responsible for integration in its particular area and integration has to be applied to all areas of policy (Bakbasel, 2012[5]). The Ministry of Justice (responsible for migration, asylum, residence permits) and the Ministry of Employment (responsible for employment, establishment, integration through work) are the two state departments responsible for most of the migration and integration policies. The Equality Ombudsman (DO) is in charge of overseeing discrimination laws. Sweden has intensified efforts to combat discrimination of foreign-born individuals since the 1990s. A comprehensive law against all kinds of discrimination was introduced in 2009. It is impossible, according to some studies, to determine whether these measures have begun to reduce discrimination (DELMI, 2017[15]).

Principle of universal access to public services, with a significant exception:

The guiding principle of integration politics is that the school system, welfare provisions, labour integration and health care are accessible to all societal groups on the same basis. However, this breaks with past national policies. In particular, since 1968 education policy provided for educating pupils in the general school system in their mother tongue (Mother tongue reform), in early 2000s the system switched to Swedish as the universal language of education for all students.

Currently, few policies are in place for migrants in areas such as: orientation of newly arrived immigrants (particularly refugees), naturalisation and citizenship, discrimination, human rights, spatial segregation and monitoring of progress (Bakbasel, 2012[5]).

The government action specifically targeting refugees is combined under a comprehensive multifaceted package called the "Introduction Programme" implemented since 2010 under the aegis of the Public Employment Service (PES) – in Swedish Arbetsformedlingen-.

This highly-developed programme of targeted integration activities (see details in section 2.4.1) has provided the template for integration systems across many OECD countries (OECD, 2016[4]). Since 2010, the main responsibility for the introduction of new arrivals was moved with this programme from municipalities to the central PES. According to evaluations (DELMI, 2017[15]), this has strengthened the labour market aspect of the introduction programme, making efforts more uniform across the country. At the same time, this reduced the possibility for tailored initiatives for the new arrivals at the local level.

Multi-level principle

In Sweden, nearly all redistributive tasks have been devolved from the central government to counties and municipalities. This makes overall co-ordination capacity, proper incentives, and fiscal equalisation, critical for policy success (OECD, 2017[9]). This is particularly true with respect to ensuring equitable access to welfare for all vulnerable groups, including migrants. Integration is mainstreamed into the policies at national level and is reinforced through the institutions of the general welfare system and through sequential steps and processes (Olwig 2011: 180; Eastmond 2011; Diedrich & Styhre 2015) involving the lower levels of government such as counties and municipalities. The institutional mapping (Figure 4.1) describes the multi-level relations between the main actors involved in reception and integration of migrants and refugees. In the absence of a National integration strategy, beyond the introduction programme, the capacity of the national level to disseminate integration goals and standards across sectors and levels of government in Sweden remains limited (OECD, 2014[16]). For instance, the existence of a national integration policy, formulated in consultation with all levels of government, could help rationalise investments at different scales and could influence standards in policies such as education, health, spatial planning in order to have a coherent "integration articulation". In particular, such systems could be implemented through coherent integration indicators across levels.

Figure 2.1. Institutional Mapping for the City of Gothenburg

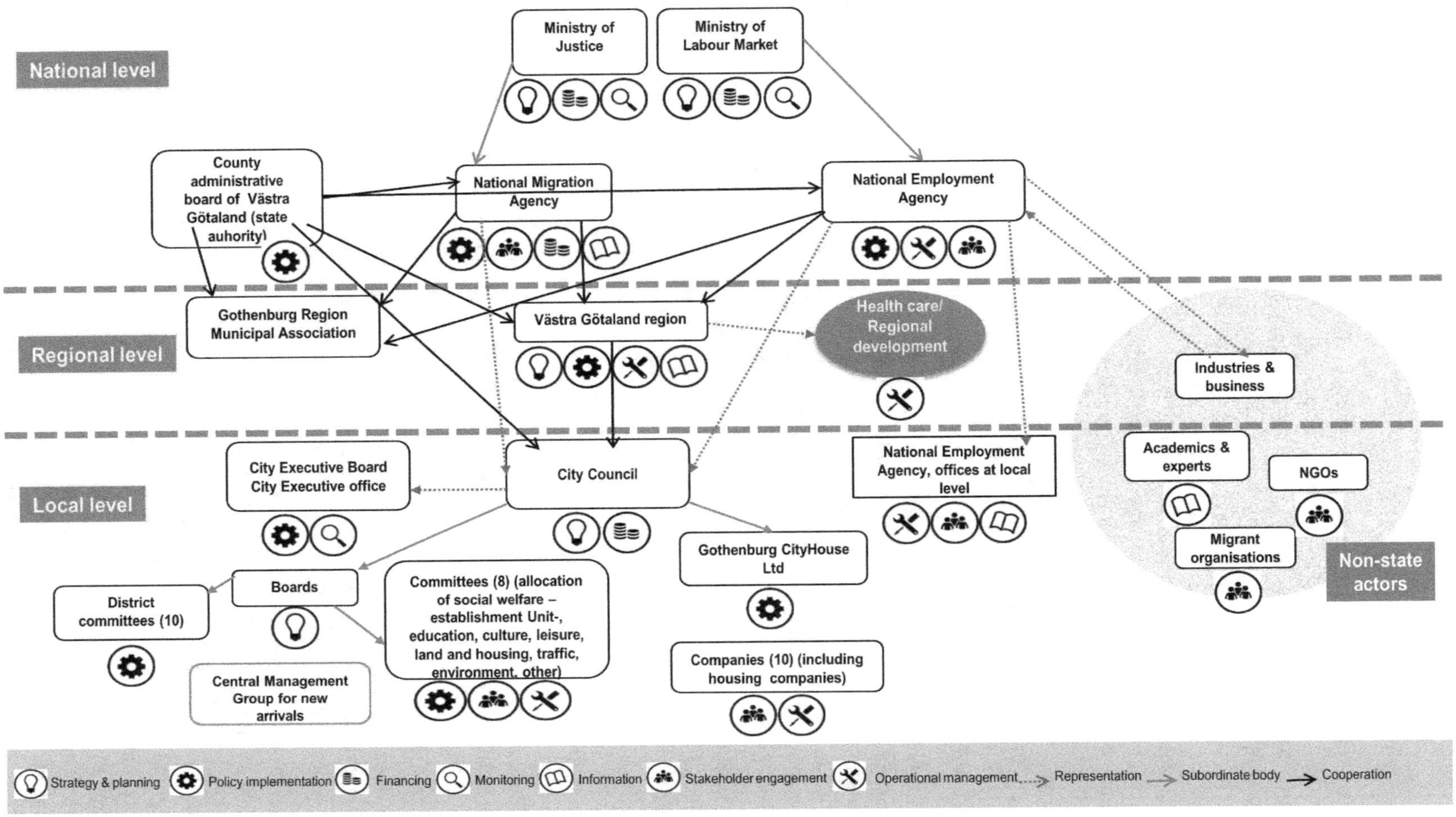

Source: Author elaboration.

County governments (Länsstyrelsen)

In Sweden, there are 21 county governments. County administrative boards govern the counties as part of the deconcentrated national administration (OECD, 2017[17]). With regard to migration, county governments support the municipalities in receiving unaccompanied children and in coordinating educational activities in Swedish and in societal orientation. County governments also distribute state grants to municipalities for reception of refugees and facilitating housing. From 1 January 2017, the county governments are also responsible for what is called "early initiatives" for asylum seekers, which is designed to make a more efficient use of the period of time they wait for asylum decisions to be made (Länsstyrelsen 2017). The Swedish Migration Agency transferred to County governments the responsibility for organising activities that aim to improve asylum seekers' skills in Swedish, enhance their knowledge of the Swedish society or the labour market or access to health.

Region Västra Götaland (Västra Götalandsregionen)

Västra Götalandsregionen is a County Council and it is composed of 49 municipalities. These 49 municipalities are divided into four intraregional associations (can be translated as municipal association or local authorities) – the Göteborg Regional Association, Fyrbodal, Skaraborg and Sjuhärad. One of the municipalities in the Göteborg Regional Association, Kungsbacka, is a part of a different region (Region Halland). So, 12 of the municipalities in the Göteborg Regional Association are part of Region Västra Götaland.

In Sweden, County councils (Landsting) are directly-elected regional bodies mainly responsible for health care and public transport. Ten out of 20 County Councils, including Vastra, also have additional responsibilities such as regional development (OECD, 2017[17]). The region does not have a remit regarding migration or immigration, but is actively involved in facilitating the establishment of newcomers and has a major responsibility when it comes to health care. The region further cooperates with both Länsstyrelsen to implement their early initiatives, and with all 49 of the municipalities on a wide array of integration projects including health, public health, culture and information spreading, often by providing a certain amount of funding.

Municipal Level

The local level is a significant stakeholder in the Swedish political system and municipalities, responsible for housing and schooling, have traditionally played a leading role in integration. This role has evolved throughout the modern history of Sweden.

Since the national mother tongue reform introduced in 1976, municipalities have been in charge of providing primary and upper-secondary education to pupils' in the general school system in their mother tongue. This policy was subsequently abolished and migrant students are taught in Swedish at school. Municipalities remained in charge of designing integration policies according to needs, offering state funded language and labour market training as well as social care. In 1991, there was a shift in the funding model and the state reimbursed municipalities on a per person basis for a period of two years from the time of the newcomers' arrival as opposed to reimbursement of costs for social assistance, which created an incentive to help newcomers become self-sufficient as quickly as possible (Emilsson, 2015[18]). Since 2010, these integration measures have been grouped under the 'Introduction programme' and are, for the majority, centrally managed by PES. For a thorough description of the Introduction Programme refer to section 2.1.3 and 2.4.1 as well as to previous OECD work (OECD, 2016[11]). As discussed in this chapter, the introduction activities rely on multi-level governance coordination between the actors involved in the provision of services.

In addition, municipalities traditionally decided whether they were ready to host and provide for refugees – being responsible for housing, language classes and other integration measures - but since 2017 the decision on how many refugees they can host has been centralised and municipalities are obliged to receive and provide accommodation to the number of refugees allocated by the central government (for a more detailed breakdown of competences regarding refugees' reception and integration see section 2.1.3).

Box 2.1. Examples of coordination across sectors and levels of government in Sweden

- Sweden has experimented with a number of national-local dialogue mechanisms for different policy sectors. Examples of coordination mechanisms involving integration issues are listed below. The National Forum on Regional Competitiveness, Entrepreneurship and Employment (renamed Forum for Sustainable Growth and Regional Attractiveness), under the Ministry of enterprise and innovation, was established in 2007 and serves as a platform for ongoing political dialogue between civil servants from national and regional levels (director level) and a second group involving national and regional level politicians. This forum supports the implementation of the National Strategy for Sustainable Regional Growth and Attractiveness (2015-2020), which also serves to combine EU and state funding to invest in key enabling factors. It includes, for instance, a plan to implement EU rural development funds (OECD, Territorial review Sweden, 2017). It meets to discuss issues such as competence allocation or thematic issues, for example on immigration, offering the opportunity for regions to present their experiences, through a "regional lens" for considering initiatives in this sector (OECD, Multi-level governance reforms: overview of OECD country experiences, 2017). In parallel, Sweden has strengthened the dialogue on urban development by setting up a formalised forum for dialogue. The National Platform for Sustainable Urban Development was launched in 2014 and aims at co-ordinating the stakeholders of sustainable urban development, including special purpose agencies, ministries, etc. As an example of actions implemented through this platform, urban environment agreements are being prepared to boost investments in urban public transport. Additional support is given to the municipalities to combat segregation and improve living conditions (OECD, OECD Regional Outlook 2016: productive regions for inclusive societies, 2016). Specific topics such as migrant integration could be addressed through this mechanism.

- An example of multi-level coordination mechanism at regional level is the Sustainable Development Advisory Committee (Beredningen för hållbar utveckling) between Region Västra Götaland and its constituent municipalities. The BHU discusses issues such as infrastructure, culture, environment and climate, industry and the private sector, research and development and skills and training development. This not a decision-making body but allows municipalities to identify issues where cooperation and synergies are possible. This cooperation is the basis for some decisions made by the regional government in some strategic issues that are relevant to sustainable development. During 2015-2016, for example, the BHU received updates from various stakeholders (including the Migration Agency, the County Administrative Board, and the municipalities) on how each was working with the question of integrating new arrivals and refugees, and discussed this issue in terms of sustainable development in the region (Information provided by Gothenburg municipality).

Interaction with neighbour municipalities to reach effective scale in social infrastructure and service delivery to migrants and refugees

The 49 municipalities in Region Västra Götaland are divided into four intraregional associations (can be translated as municipal association or local authorities) – the Göteborg Regional Association, Fyrbodal, Skaraborg and Sjuhärad.

Gothenburg Regional Association[1] is an organisation tasked with fostering cooperation between 13 municipalities in the region. The association coordinates municipalities on issues related to infrastructure and traffic (e.g. the creation of the congestion tax). As the number of refugees and asylum seekers increased and the law making refugee reception mandatory for municipalities (please see more details in paragraph 4.3.2) went into effect in March 2016, the association has played a role in coordinating and supporting municipalities' efforts to welcome and integrate these groups. Since 2015, the Chief Executives of the 13 municipalities have met every week to discuss measures pertaining to the distribution and integration of refugees. The 2016 law clarified local tasks and targets for reception and integration and made collaboration across municipalities increasingly necessary.

"Municipalities from the region had to change the way they worked together, enlarging the scale of city planning to neighbouring municipalities and taking collectively the responsibility to welcome refugees." (City Councillor for the city of Lerum, Region Vastra Gotaland)

Municipalities in the Gothenburg region cooperate with each other on various measures for new arrivals, in areas such as education in Swedish (SFI), societal orientation, housing and rehabilitation. For instance, the Association Board was in charge of leading the tender for buying modular homes for asylum seekers in the different municipalities. Specific courses for newcomers could be difficult to arrange in every municipality (e.g. vocational training with language support). These regional arrangements allow new arrivals to access these measures regardless of which municipality they live in, and to continue – in case they move on to another municipality within the region – to benefit from such measures. One purpose is to make it more attractive and easier to move between municipalities (e.g. from Gothenburg to the other municipalities in the region and vice versa) as all social orientation courses are given in central Gothenburg, which enables all newly arrived individuals to visit the city centre on a regular basis. Municipalities included in the association also cooperate in finding placement and housing for unaccompanied minors. This type of horizontal co-operation is well rooted in Sweden where inter-municipal co-operation in public service delivery has existed since 1919 when municipalities and counties had the opportunity to form local federations, a special local authority to which members can transfer the management of some municipal competences (OECD, 2017[19]).

The labour market situation in the Vastra Gotaland region varies across localities, several municipalities in the region are becoming depopulated. It is critical to create incentives for newcomers to settle in other municipalities in the region apart from Gothenburg (Meeting with Gothenburg Regional Association, municipality of Gothenburg 16 March 2017). For example, a joint venture at work for newcomers with an engineering education has been developed by the association (Additional information provided by the City Executive Office, 23 May 2017).

Objective 2 Seek policy coherence in addressing multi-dimensional migrant needs at the local level

City vision and approach to integration

The city of Gothenburg implements governmental integration policies without a specific strategy for integration at city level. In the past, the city had a targeted approach: the municipality was involved in providing pupils' education in their mother tongue and funding directly migrants' local associations (for more details see paragraph 2.1.2. Information from the OECD questionnaire completed by the city of Gothenburg, 2017).

Currently, integration is seen as part of the city's social sustainability. Given the high inequalities registered among inhabitants (as described in Section 1.4), the main objective of the city is more sustainable inclusion and a foreword-looking strategy has been developed since 2014 "Reducing *Inequality in living conditions and health in Gothenburg*" (box 4.2). This multifaceted local strategy encompasses integration, which is expected to happen through several dimensions compared to the integration through labour, which is pursued through the national Introduction programme. In addition, the city has developed a framework against segregation and has also identified increased participation, support and collaboration with civil society as priorities (OECD meeting with the municipality 16 March 2017).

The city's social sustainability remit is clearly set out in the budget, where the overall planning for the municipality is defined. Since 2013 and again in 2015, the city of Gothenburg included a number of prioritised objectives in the budget, focusing on reducing inequalities in living conditions and health and creating good opportunities in life for everyone (Gothenburg, 2014[3]). The municipal budget of 2016 inserts an explicit goal of addressing issues related to racism as well as segregation and socio-economic inequalities (*Budget 2016*).

Particularly in the absence of operational integration policies, these substantive goals for long-term inclusion have to be coupled by day-to-day efforts of all public services for ensuring equitable access for migrants to universal service provision. This is a challenging task and needs close monitoring. In Gothenburg, in the view of some of the NGOs operating in this sector (see section 2.2) access to public services is differentiated for each category of migrants based on their legal status and this sometimes makes the system complex to navigate by the users. Migrants have to learn a new system every time their status changes and they easily find themselves in a loophole where they temporarily don't belong to any 'box' and their access to services might be suspended. Services attached to each status are often decided by national regulations. However, the municipality can act at the margin of these regulations and can take a 'road map' approach to ensure migrants have access to information about the services they are entitled to. When needed, they can orient them to non-state organisations that can reach the persons who are not covered by the public systems.

> **Box 2.2. Equal Gothenburg a strategy for a socially sustainable city**
>
> The Management Group for a socially sustainable city comprises all ten district directors as well as the director of the Committee for Allocation of Social Welfare of the city of Gothenburg (see paragraph 4.2.1). It published a report entitled 'Inequality in living conditions and health in Gothenburg' (Gothenburg, 2014), which provides a description of the disparities in living conditions between different groups and districts and proposes policy measures in four focal areas: i) Give every child a good start in life; ii) provide children with good conditions throughout their school years; iii) create preconditions for work and iv) create sustainable environments and communities that promote health. The strategy Equal Gothenburg has been prepared around these focal areas and is detailed with 30 proposals and 130 examples of what Gothenburg can do: 'the idea is that these proposals should stimulate discussion about what the City ought to do, wants to do and can do in order to reduce inequality in Gothenburg' (Gothenburg, 2014). In January 2018 the City Council voted the programme for Equal Gothenburg. The Committee for allocation of social welfare who coordinates the work has the task to translate it into an action plan for which 10 million SEK have been allocated. However measures and resources for implementing most of the actions are expected to be derived also through regular committees' operations and budgets.

City institutional setting with relevance for migrant integration

In administrative terms, the inner city is divided into ten districts (*stadsdelsnämnder*), in turn split into primary units and altogether 900 "basic areas". The districts take decisions on, for example, preschool, primary school, social care, and care for the elderly. Greater Gothenburg, includes other municipalities, making up what is called the Göteborg Regional Association with the exception of Kungsbacka.[2]

Since 2014 elections, Gothenburg has been run by a coalition of three parties: the Social Democrats, the Environmental Party, the Left and Feminist Initiative. The budget's focus is primarily on socioeconomic issues.

Currently (figure 4.2), the Gothenburg municipality is organised in Committees (for allocation of social welfare, for education, culture, leisure, land and housing, technical supply, traffic, environment and other boards) and each committee is governed by a board. The Committees are independent from the city Executive Board.

The City executive office works on policy issues regarding the city's assignments and activities. It also coordinates and monitors the work of the city in terms of management and company compliance. The Management Office contributes to reaching a consensus and adopting a holistic view of the city's multiple political directions. The office evaluates the basis for goal fulfilment, for example. The City executive office contains specialists in different fields, such as migration, integration and refugee reception. The City executive office also has a department that works with issues regarding human rights and national minorities. Its assignment includes educating and supporting the different branches of the city's administrations in this work.

In addition, there are a number of municipally owned companies, all owned by Gothenburg CityHouse limited.

Figure 2.2. Organisation of the municipality of Gothenburg

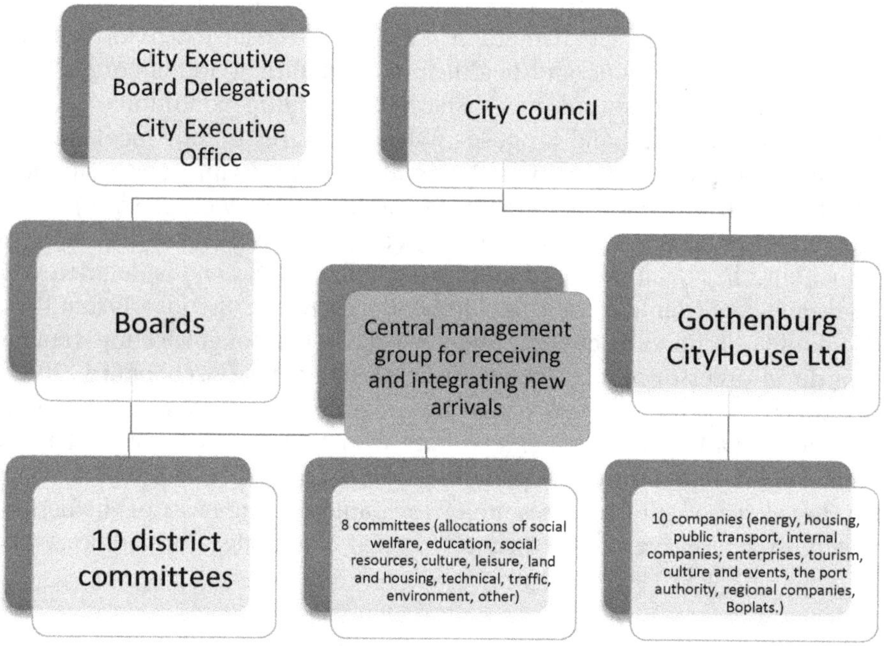

Source: Created by the authors based on information provided by the municipality

Relevant administrations for migrant integration

In line with national policy and organisation, integration is considered a responsibility across all areas of the municipal level, and thus there is no integration department. It is worth noting that in the 1970s, the municipality established an Interpreter and migrant service. In the early 1980s, the municipality created a Special Board for Migrant Issues, where the majority of the members had a migration background (Information from the OECD questionnaire completed by the city of Gothenburg, 2017). The board was responsible for the Interpreter and migrant services, financial support to migrant organisations and religious communities and had the task of developing information and skills with regard to immigration and integration issues for municipal employees and the general public. The board was also responsible for various national/municipal projects in the field of health (such as projects targeting HIV/AIDS and combatting female circumcision), special measures to encourage migrant participation in elections and society in general. The board, as well as the Interpreter and migrant service was phased out in 2000 and its activities were transferred to other municipal boards.

Boards that are more involved on migrant-related issues include: the Board for sports and associations that often funds migrant associations' activities, the Board of culture that funds cultural events promoting intercultural dialogue and inclusive cultural life and the Board for Allocation of Social Welfare, a body providing support to the districts for issues related to social benefits and safety. This board manages a fund for social and integration promotion activities to which NGOs can apply.

Within this office the Establishment Unit, provides support for the newly arrived within the framework of the national Introduction programme. This section is specific to the city of Gothenburg and works in cooperation with the PES to help eligibly people as well as their relatives and unaccompanied minors. This unit works as One-stop-shop for refugees and is funded by local budget that gets contribution from the national level for reception of refugees. Refugees receive help filling their application for the housing, information on how it works and about other opportunities available in the cities. The establishment unit also relies on social workers who are bilingual and use external interpreters on daily basis. This unit respond to refugee needs during the first two years since they establish in the city. After that time, if they are still in need of assistance they can rely on the services of the district where they reside. The establishment unit doesn't have the task of coordinating the activities of all other departments around integration issues.

The Integration centre a one-stop-shop for migrants (see section 2.2) is also part of the Committee for allocation of social resources.

In addition, the implementation of Equal Gothenburg is also relevant for integration-related issues. The Committee of allocation of social welfare is in charge of drawing an action plan for the program for Equal Gothenburg that was voted by the City Council in January 2018. The programme is part of the city's budget (10 million SEK), therefore each goal is reported to the City Executive Board and the City Council.

City coordination around integration-relevant issues

All municipal committees and administrations have a responsibility to contribute to achieving social sustainability. The City Executive Office monitors the work of committees and boards through the budget[3], following-up regularly how all goals are implemented. It also has the opportunity to ask specific questions to the city's committees and boards when is needed. Although there is no specific integration target for integration, there is a human rights goal that states that all the city's activities should be permeated by human rights.

Since 2014/2015 the city has set up a permanent Management Group for receiving and integrating new arrivals, consisting of heads of units of different boards (housing, education and labour market, social affairs). The aim is to make the reception and integration of newcomers as effective and smooth as possible, through a shared action plan. The Management Group doesn't have a budget but the City Executive Office has approximately SEK 2 million for coordination of the city's reception of new arrivals. One of the objectives of the Management Group is to create a structured cooperation with NGOs on reception of newcomers.

Multi-level governance of asylum seekers and refugees reception and integration mechanisms

Asylum seekers and refugee regulation

Sweden has historically been known for implementing one of the most generous asylum policies in the EU. For instance, from 2013, all Syrian asylum seekers received permanent residence permits. However, in relation to the situation in 2014-2015, Sweden updated its asylum policy. Several restrictive reforms were implemented in 2016 and Sweden now applies only minimal EU standards (Migration Agency 2016). The legislation introduced the following main changes:

- residence permits for refugees are now limited to three years (Lag (2016:752)): if there are still reasons for protection when the permit expires, a prolonged permit may be granted. If the person is able to support her/himself, a permanent permit of residence may be granted.

- residence permits for those holding a subsidiary protection status - according to EU standards[4] - are limited to 13 months (Lag (2016:752)) (OECD International Migration Outlook 2017, Sweden). The limited permits can be prolonged and if reasons for protection continue and if the person is capable of providing for oneself, a permanent permit can be provided.
- Family reunification is restricted. Refugees with temporary residence permit can apply for family reunification. For persons recognised as being in need of subsidiary protection after the 24 November 2015, family reunification is only allowed as an exception[5]. For family reunification, there are also requirements including being able to support oneself and having access to housing (Lag 2016:752; OECD International Migration Outlook 2017, Sweden).
- An asylum-seeker who no longer has the right to economic support or accommodation if he or she has received a decision of expulsion or rejection, or if the time for voluntary return after a rejection of an asylum seeking application has expired.
- Assessment of age is to be implemented earlier in the asylum seeking process (Ds 2016:37). This provision has consequences for the municipality's work with unaccompanied minors (see further below).

Dispersal mechanisms for Asylum seekers and refugees

The Swedish Migration Agency (under the Ministry of Justice) is responsible for basic sustenance and accommodation for asylum seekers – i.e. the Law on reception of asylum seekers (Lag 1994: 137), from registration to the time when the decision on the asylum application is made. Accommodation of asylum seekers, aside from unaccompanied minors, can be arranged by the Migration Agency in rental apartments, hotel rooms, camping cottages, modular components, or other solutions. The Migration Agency identifies availability of these structures across the country and County administrative boards have agreements with municipalities on the number of asylum seekers that each one has to take. There is a dialogue with national authorities regarding the presence of asylum seeker hosting facilities but the presence and number of asylum seekers is not negotiable. The asylum seekers can choose to provide their own accommodation (see box 4.3). If unable to provide for themselves – when applying for asylum one must inform the Migration Agency of any potential assets –asylum seekers can receive a daily allowance paid by the Migration Agency. In 2017, the daily allowance was SEK 24 (€2.5) for adults alone staying at accommodations where food is provided and SEK 12 for each child until 17 years of age, and SEK 71 a day when food is not provided, or if accommodation has been organised by the asylum seeker her/himself, and an additional sum for children, varying in relation to age. Municipalities have to ensure asylum seekers children the possibility to attend schools. Adults have the possibility to participate in Swedish courses and language cafes, organized by voluntary organizations. NGOs receive compensation for arranging courses.

With regards to status holders, the dispersal system between 1992 and 2016 relied on municipalities. Municipalities were able to decide for themselves how many refugees they were prepared to receive through agreements with the county. Until 2010, they were also in charge of organising all measures related to settlement (e.g. housing, language lessons (SFI Swedish for immigrants), translation etc.) and received from the state a lump-sum per capita disbursement calculated to cover integration costs. Since the 2010

Introduction Act (see section 2.4.1), the PES has been mandate with helping permits holders get settled, allocating them across counties on the basis of local labour market opportunities, population size and the number of asylum seekers living in the Migration Agency facilities. In practice however, given that the PES owns no accommodations themselves, the PES was heavily dependent on the municipalities to offer available housing and rarely accessed housing in the area surrounding the larger cities (OECD, Working Together: Skills and Labour Market Integration of Immigrants and their children in Sweden, 2016). Past financial incentives for refugee settlement failed to encourage municipalities, who find the funding insufficient for the investments needed to house more newcomers.

Due to large variations in municipality willingness to receive refugees, and to increasing numbers of recognised refugees waiting in the Migration Agency's reception system to be assigned to accommodation (14 000 at the end of 2015) in a municipality, the dispersal system for status holders changed with the introduction of the Reception for Settlement Act in 1 March 2016. This system applies to those status holders who apply for assistance to find permanent housing (refugees have the option to find their own accommodation see box 4.3). The migration agency assigns the refugee to a municipality of destination – where he/she receives a personal identity number (personnummer) from the Local Tax office. Since 2017, municipalities must receive and organise accommodation for refugees who have acquired a residence permit and for resettled refugees, in order to make responsibilities more evenly spread across the country (Riksdagen 2016). The Act doesn't specify for how many years municipalities have to provide accommodation to the refugees who are assigned to their localities, which remains municipal discretion.

Beginning in 2017, a formula negotiated by the Migration Agency, the Association of local authorities and Regions and the Public Employment Service (PES) assigns protection beneficiaries to each of the 21 counties in Sweden based on total population, existing number of protection beneficiaries in the county and labour market conditions (Fratzke, 2017[20]). It is then the County Government who makes the decision on the numbers of newly arrived individuals who are to be received by each municipality within a county. The County redistributes the refugees across municipalities based on a number of considerations, including the conditions of the local labour market, the number of migrants already in the municipality, and housing availability.

In 2016, the work was carried out on the basis of a detailed planning of the reception, also for the 1 900 resettled refugees that Sweden received during 2016, in each municipality, which was developed in cooperation with the Swedish Public Employment Service. In 2017, the Swedish Migration Agency took over the task of settlement assignment from the Public Employment Agency (Swedish Migration agency, 2017[21]).

This dispersion criterion is an interesting attempt to avoid over-concentration in cities and second movements of newcomers by distributing them where there are labour supply shortages. This mechanism should also be assessed for its capacity to bring status holders closer to their families as well as to attractive labour markets, now that all cities have to live up to their obligation to find housing solutions for the individuals assigned to their localities. However, this obligatory system still relies on the capacities of the municipalities to find appropriate housing for refugees, which was the main bottleneck in the previous mechanism. For instance, within the framework of the OECD Småland Blekinge territorial review (OECD, 2017[9]) it was reported that, while the county administrative boards have agreements with municipalities on the number of refugees that each has to take, many municipalities do not have adequate housing and as such, have not fulfilled these obligations. Instead, in some cases, they prefer to pay other municipalities to settle their asylum seekers. More information on Gothenburg solutions for housing refugees can be found in paragraph 7.2.

In 2017 Gothenburg received approximately 3000 refugees. Of these 1100 were assigned by the Swedish Migration Board, the other refugees have arranged accommodation on their own, many staying with friends and relatives. In 2018, approximately 2 300 refugees are expected to be received in Gothenburg. About 700 of these will be assigned by the Swedish Migration Board. There seems to be room for improving the communication mechanism between national and local levels, with regards to refugee dispersal. Since 2014, the Gothenburg municipality perceived the national policy as more difficult to predict, and felt an important amount of pressure was put on the municipalities, and was not always accompanied by visibility on future funding (OECD interviews with the City council representative, 16 March 2017).

Box 2.3 Swedish double reception system for asylum seekers and refugees based on their choice

Since 1994, a new Law on "organising independent living" was introduced. It allowed asylum seekers, during the time it takes for the asylum process to be handled, to choose between institutionalised accommodation ABO (anordnat boende) provided by the National Migration Agency or to organise living arrangements by themselves IBO (egenordnat boende). See paragraph 2.1.3 for more details on the allowance provided with this accommodation. From 1986 and 1994 a compulsory dispersion policy was introduced to avoid over-concentration of immigrants in few regions but the policy fell short of linking settlement locations with the local labour market's needs. The result was migrants having to move a second time (Bakbasel, 2012). Since this option was made available, many asylum seekers choose to organise their own accommodation. As of March 2017, more than half of asylum applicants in Sweden were living in assisted housing facilities (called ABO accommodation) while nearly 30% had found their own accommodation. The remaining 20% primarily includes unaccompanied minors who were housed in other types of facilities (Migration, 2017).

This option is also available for status holder who can decide to find their own accommodation and in Sweden in 2016 only 45% of status holders required assistance (OECD, Working Together: Skills and Labour Market Integration of Immigrants and their children in Sweden, 2016).

Traditionally most of the asylum seekers and status holders who arrive in Gothenburg have chosen the option to organise their living arrangements and are hosted by relatives or friends. They tend to locate in neighbourhoods where the existing diaspora are located, often outside of the city centre, either in the Northeast, in Biskopsgården (Hisingen) or Frölunda/Tynnered. They often live in crowded conditions (Evidens 2017), and for many families and children the conditions are poor (Göteborgs stad, 2013). Some of them sublease apartments on the black market (Ibid: 24). For instance, the official figure of inhabitants in Angered is 51 000, but district officials estimate that the actual number is an additional 10 000 consisting of asylum seekers (Meeting with district official, Angered 17 March 2017). In the view of some representatives from civil society organisations as well as social workers from the municipality, expressed during interviews with the OECD, the possibility for asylum seekers to organise accommodations by themselves makes the system more complex and might lower the standards and protection of the accommodation offered to this group. Since 2005, recognising potential drawbacks of choosing their own accommodation in terms of segregation, overcrowding and poor social integration, the government stopped incentivising status holders and asylum seekers using this option, while still making it an option (OECD, Working Together: Skills and Labour Market Integration of Immigrants and their children in Sweden, 2016). However, it is observed that due to the length on average of the completion of the settlement process including, in 2016, 125 days on average for granting a residence permit and a further delay of 163 days until the person is permanently settled in a municipality – half of the refugees who initially decided to seek assistance in finding housing finally opted for not accepting the municipality they had been assigned by the PES and to look for their own accommodation, losing their right to receive assistance for finding permanent housing (OECD, Working Together: Skills and Labour Market Integration of Immigrants and their children in Sweden, 2016).

Unaccompanied minors and vulnerable migrants

With regards to asylum-seeking unaccompanied minors, there is a shared responsibility between the state and the municipal level. All municipalities are obliged to receive unaccompanied minors and to provide for accommodation and schooling opportunities. Sometimes, they are placed in individual family homes, but more often in Homes for care or accommodation (HVB)[6]. The municipality is responsible for running such homes, often organised in empty school buildings, or other official buildings that are renovated into institutional homes. Trained staff are available in these houses to provide counselling and activities.

In June 2017, a change in the law came into effect, for young people who arrived after 24 November 2015. Now the age test happens earlier in the registration process and more restrictive conditions for protection status (residence permits 3 years and 13 months for those with subsidiary protection) apply for those assessed as being older than 18 years old. The law also allows young people, arrived prior to 24 November 2015, who studied in secondary schooling to receive a residence permit that are valid for four years.

Children and young unaccompanied adults are at particular risk of psychological troubles in relation to fears of being expelled and when they change from municipal custody to the Migration Agency system, if they are defined as older than they claim. Once unaccompanied minors are defined as being 18 or actually turn 18 years old, they are no longer under municipal responsibility and are accommodated by the Migration agency in shelters for adults. This often implies losing the social network where they were embedded, including schools. At age 18, the individual also loses the right to be accompanied by the trustee (*god man)*. The trustee represents the child in the asylum-seeking process and other official matters. In this delicate passage from unaccompanied minor facilities to Migration Agency systems, an undefined number of unaccompanied minors who just turned or are defined as above 18 years old try to return to live in Gothenburg and sometimes end up on the street. Some non-governmental organisations, such as Agape, a church-based organisation, have organised voluntary work primarily to find accommodation for these young people, but also to organise support structures in other ways. Until mid-March 2017, Agape had found new homes for 65 kids. There is no official funding, but Agape runs a donor's campaign in order to finance, for example, the rental of apartments (OECD Meetings with civil society organisations, health care personnel, 15-16 March 2017). A new network labelled #wecan'tstandit (*#vistårinteut)*, based on professionals meeting vulnerable youth has also been created in order to provide practical and political support to at risk, unaccompanied minors.

Objective 3. Ensure access to, and effective use of, financial resources that are adapted to local responsibilities for migrant integration

At the national level, the National Migration Agency and the Employment Agency are the two main actors managing funding for integration and migration issues. In 2016, these two agencies received increased national contributions for handling applications and enhancement of integration measures (the Migration Agency received an increase of 2017 financial result of €56 million or 1,1% of its budget which is 4,7 billion EUR). The funds are directed towards skill assessment and validation for asylum seekers, language training, reforms regarding the syllabus and organisation of Swedish for Immigrants as well as a fast track programme for entrepreneurs (OECD International Migration Outlook, Sweden).

Municipalities receive grants to compensate for their responsibility to accommodate asylum seekers and refugees. The County governments (Länsstyrelsen) have the responsibility to redistribute national government grants to the municipalities from the Migration board. In 2015, 34% (GP 2016) of Gothenburg's costs for integration measures were covered by central government grants. It is estimated that central government compensation for reception of refugees amounted to SEK 360 million in 2017; and will amount to SEK 390 million in 2018. The City Executive Office has approximately SEK 2 million for coordination of the city's reception of new arrivals.

Additionally, the city of Gothenburg received SEK 123 million for strengthening housing capacity, which the City executive council believes is insufficient (OECD interviews with Gothenburg Municipality, March 2017).

Transfers from the PES to the municipalities for the Introduction Programme are channelled through the Migration Board. The introduction benefit, including the living and housing allocations to which recognised refugees are entitled during the first two years, is co-ordinated by the PES and paid by the Social Insurance Agency and distributed by the municipality to each beneficiary (see section 2.4.3). Previous analysis observed that this time-bounded compensation might not be reflective of the actual needs for integration that the municipality has to address, particularly for those newcomers who have lower levels of qualification and skills and take longer to find employment, despite distribution mechanisms that are more reflective of market needs. After the first two years, no more targeted funding is transferred to municipalities for their work with migrants (OECD, 2016[11]). A more comprehensive approach to national support to local authorities could take into account that, depending on the characteristics of the migrant population, municipalities will have to provide welfare subsidies to those who did not find a job at the end of the Introduction programme. In addition the municipality noted that efforts for receiving newcomers are better compensated in some sectors than others. For instance, for the education sector, national compensation is sufficient for additional teaching resources but does not cover the full cost of an education site (Information provided during OECD interviews with the Municipality of Gothenburg).

Public transfers related to refugees and asylum seekers have to be put in the broader context of well decentralised spending[7] characterising Sweden, which scores within the five most decentralised countries in the OECD with regards to spending. Sweden's sub-national governments are responsible for 49.1% of public expenditure (OECD, 2016[22]). Local authorities have a significant margin in designing and implementing local integration measures thanks to a variety of mechanisms (e.g. co-operative capacities, municipal enterprises, access to credit, etc.). While subnational authorities are currently reasonably well equipped financially to meet their high level of task and expenditure responsibilities[8], the recent OECD territorial review highlighted how new concerns, linked to the integration of migrants and asylum seekers in the labour market, skills development and pressures on the housing supply have also become important challenges for local budgets (OECD, 2017[9]).

EU financing mechanisms across levels of the government

Actors at different levels of the government – national, regional and municipal –work with specific EU financing tools in order to foster inclusion.

In West Sweden, the EU funds belong to the "Structural Fund Partnership" (SFP) which has its secretariat in the region of Västra Götaland[9]. SFP consists of elected representatives for local and regional level (currently a member from the city of

Gothenburg is represented), representatives of the civil society, labour market, social economy as well as national authorities assigned by the Swedish government. The SFP has the assignment to prioritize and award funding to the submitted applications to both the European Social Fund and the European Regional Development Fund, as well as to coordinate calls for proposals based on specific regional needs or intentions. The national agencies the Swedish ESF Council (ESF) and The Swedish Agency for Economic and Regional Growth (ERDF) are in charge of management and distribution of these funds but are bound by SFP prioritization.

Between 2007 and 2013, EU-funded projects amounted to a total of €45 million for 800 projects. The projects were funded through the European Regional Development Fund (ERDF)[10] and the European Social Fund (ESF)[11]. Most funding relating to integration is found in ESF's second priority area "Increasing transitions to work" ("Öka övergångarna till arbete")[12] which is focused on making it easier for youth (15–24 years), long-term unemployed (more than 12 months), people with functional impairments, newly arrived migrants and long-term sick leavers to obtain employment or improve their chances of getting a job. Examples include education and training, work placement and job matching, vocational training and preparatory initiatives, for example validation of skills. The Employment Agency is often a partner in ESF projects and helps identify beneficiaries, including newcomers or immigrants (information provided by the City Executive Office, 9 May 2017; Additional information provided by the Västra Götaland region, 23 May 2017).

The level of financing from these funds varies. Projects financed through funds administered by the Agency for Economic and Regional Growth can be funded (up to 40% of the total costs), while funding from the ESF Council can be as high as 75% of the total costs[13].

Another interesting example of EU funds management mechanism is the ITI or Integrated Territorial Investments[14] a voluntary EU instrument introduced 2014 for managing the European cohesion policy and applies to West Sweden ERDF programme regards sustainable urban development in Gothenburg. ITI supports multilevel co-operation and co-ordination of actions in order to achieve shared multi-dimensional goals such as sustainable urban development. Within the framework of the ITI the Executive Committee of Gothenburg formulated a cross-sectoral action plan for ERDF investments in the city, including possible urban development projects as well as municipal key policies for this purpose i. e. environment, equality and urban planning. The action plan is part of the West Sweden ERDF programme and 4.8% of the West Sweden 2014-2020 budget is assigned it (2 688 832 euro requiring about four million euro from the city and partner investors). ITI/ERDF is a unique example of municipal participation in management of EU fund. The municipality is actually involvement in the programming process and evaluation of EU funds thanks to the seat in the SFP for one representative of Gothenburg Executive Committee. In addition ERDF for youth unemployment and social inclusion is managed first of all through sustainable urban development actions (ITI). Municipal authorities felt that although ESF is more focused on integration priorities, their involvement is not as strong and direct as with ERDF because ESF has only one national program instead of eight regional ERDF programmes and no ITI.

Notes

[1] One of the municipalities in the Göteborg Regional Association, Kungsbacka, is a part of a different region (Region Halland). So, 12 of the municipalities in the Göteborg Regional Association are part of Region Västra Götaland. http://www.vgregion.se/en/about/.

[2] Ale, Alingsås, Härryda, Kungsbacka, Kungälv, Lerum, Lilla Edet. Mölndal, Partille, Stenungsund, Tjörn and Öckerö. Those municipalities also make up what is called the Göteborg Regional Association of Municipalities. They are all included in the region Västra Götaland, except for Kungsbacka, which belongs to Halland.

[3] The budget decided by the municipal council – in June and interim budgets can be presented three times per year by the City Executive Office – defines goals and directions for each policy area. Goals are to be turned into practical activities and this is the task of the committees and their boards.

[4] Asylum could be granted to persons who do not qualify as 'refugees' but who face a risk of serious harm in the home country.

[5] This new temporary law, which came into effect in July 2016, means that persons who are assigned refugee status, and then a three-year residence permit, will be entitled to reunite with their nuclear family. Those who are assessed as in alternative need for protection receive temporary permits for 13 months and have very limited opportunities for family reunification.

[6] "Hem för vård eller boende" (HVB).

[7] Sweden is one of the most decentralised countries in the world in terms of public service delivery and expenditure: about 25% of the country's GDP is accounted for by subnational government expenditure, and the subnational government enjoys extensive spending, taxing and decision-making autonomy. (OECD, 2017[9])

[8] Sweden's "financing principle" eliminates the possibility of unfunded mandates for subnational governments

[9] In Sweden there are eight SFP according to NUTS2 regions

[10] Administered by the Swedish Agency for Economic and Regional Growth.

[11] Administered by the Swedish ESF Council.

[12] https://www.esf.se/Documents/In%20english/Develop%20Sweden%20info_0617_webb.pdf

[13] http://www.esf.se/Min-region/Vastsverige/Utlysningar/Kommande-utlysningar/

[14] http://ec.europa.eu/regional_policy/sources/docgener/informat/2014/iti_en.pdf

Chapter 3. Block 2. Time and proximity keys for migrants and host community to live together (Objectives 4 & 5)

This section aims to describe the leading principles along which reception and integration policies are designed at city level. Across the cities analysed in the study sample, the concepts of time and space appear to be essential in imagining durable integration solutions. Time refers to the life-long process of establishing oneself in a city, and the continuum of solutions that have to be provided along this process. Besides the objective of facilitating and hastening the integration of newcomers, cities must offer entry points for foreign born or even native born individuals with a migrant background, to facilitate the different aspects of their well-being and development throughout their lives. Space is understood as proximity and is well illustrated by the concept of *Connecting* that many cities have adopted in their approach to integration. This concept acknowledges that inclusion doesn't result automatically from living in the same city nor street, it requires sustained interaction. Cities have a role to play in encouraging such interaction, by supporting local level initiatives and creating public spaces, where connections among different groups can spark a dialogue and all components of the society (host communities, long standing migrant communities, business, third sector entities, etc.) can play their role in a multi-directional integration process.

These principles are embedded in the 30 proposals for "reducing inequality in living conditions and creating good opportunities in life for everyone" (box 4.2) of the city of Gothenburg (Gothenburg, 2014[3]), which targets vulnerabilities rather than groups based on their origins. The strategy sets out a range of multi-stakeholders, long-term measures, aiming to have well-integrated schools and reduces segregation in housing, to name just a few examples.

The aim of Strategy for a sustainable city is "To shorten distances, both between places and people. The city will be brought closer together both physically and socially. The city will be more compact with new homes, workplaces and meeting-places".(OECD meeting with the municipality 16 March 2017)

In addition to the integration-related measures in the areas attributed by law (e.g. within the Introduction programme, see box below) the city reaches beyond them within this strategy for reducing inequality. For instance, the city aims at maintaining high and equal level of quality in health, childcare, preschool and education facilities across all neighbourhoods. While measures ensuring access to universal services and medium- to long-term housing solutions will be described in section 2.4, this section highlights how the city develops places for encouraging meetings between different groups, to create linkages with a broader network of actors over time.

Spaces that foster contacts and equitable access to services over time

An example of a **space** designed to facilitate equitable access to complementary services for migrants all along their lives is the Integration Centre (*Integrationscentrum*)[1].

This section of the Committee for Allocation of social service of the city of Gothenburg, (*Social resursförvaltningen)* works as a meeting place between ''newly arrived, other migrants and Swedes''. In this centre, located in the city's downtown, the municipality organises educational and informational activities, including city tours, about Swedish society, as well as about migration. Courses in societal orientation for refugees are given by teachers with a migrant background themselves. These courses are delivered within the framework of the Introduction programme and are subsidised by the national government. In March 2017, there were 755 persons registered for training and in 2015 about 16 000 people registered. Besides seminars for skill development and workshops the centre also offers a mentoring programme – Pathfinder – to inspire newcomers to reach their professional goals. The centre also has an information office, which helps migrants in their mother tongue to fill out forms and contact authorities for key establishment issues ranging from finding accommodation to family reunification. These services are not only offered to recently arrived refugees but to all vulnerable groups including long-standing and undocumented migrants. In line with the idea that integration measures can be carried out by different players, the Integration Centre offers the opportunity for Swedes to enter into contact with migrants in their free time through the ''Refugee-guide and Language friend'' programme established in 2003. The programme brought together nearly 2 000 people in 2015 through study circles and individual meetings (OECD interviews at the Integration Centre 16 March, 2017). With the large influx of refugees in 2015, an increasing number of Swedes willing to participate in such activities and to coach refugees. Swedes volunteer to meet up with refugees, become mentors, socialise, go for walks, participate in sport activities, teach refugees to swim and women to bicycle, cooking activities, etc. The Integration centre is also a platform for cooperation with NGOs and offers migrant organisations support and training in societal orientation. This prepares them to, in turn, support newly arrived migrants (OECD Meeting with staff of the Integration Centre, 16 March 2017).

Several other grassroots initiatives run similar activities and facilitate language cafés, mentorships, buddy-systems and provide meeting places. These initiatives help establish linkages between newly arrived individuals and Swedes, facilitating informal aspects of inclusion and integration. The municipality can support associations to find spaces for organising activities in particular child, youth and sports activities. District have cultural centres and sport halls that can be hired by the associations.

In line with the idea of making spaces for integration available throughout the city, a new orientation unit, *Angeredskompassen* opened in the district of Angered (as described in section 1.2 Angered is a neighbourhood at the outskirts of the city characterised by high levels of socio-economic segregation) in 2017. Its role is to provide information for a clearer and simpler integration into Swedish society in general for newly arrived asylum seekers and their families. In this space users meet officials from all municipal sectors: Social services, Education sector, Culture & Leisure, Elderly Care services and Health Care. Different skills are grouped in this centre: teachers, social workers, leisure instructors, nurses and an administrator. The users receive individual counselling and can be directed to relevant municipal services. This unit is also in charge of running knowledge assessments of newcomers between 7-15 years old. This assessment includes language and experience, pupils' knowledge in basic school subjects including math and literacy test. Based on this information, pupils are oriented towards the relevant education institutions. The work started in early 2017, as of mid-march 79 pupils had been assessed and 18 families counselled. The intention is to work in a preventive manner and through cooperation with other actors from the district that prepare local civic orientation and leisure programmes for newcomers (Meeting with Angered district 17 March 2017).

Box 3.1. Multi-cultural city events agenda

Not only does the municipality create spaces to bring the culture "out" to the suburbs(e.g. culture houses built in the 1970s in Angered (Blå stället) and in Frölunda) but it also favours cultural activities that bring together local and migrant communities in an attempt to diversify both the content and location of cultural events. These are seen as opportunities to attract residents of Northeast districts, of which a large part has a migration background, to visit the city centre. One important event is the Kulturkalaset, a week of cultural activities at the end of the summer explicitly aimed at diversity and inclusion. Recently, for example, a music icon from the Lebanese music scene was invited. Other events that attract multi-cultural crowds are the celebrations for the Persian New year as well as the Latin American Carnival and the International film festival. Such events are often funded through a combination of municipal and private sector funding. The city museums have carried out campaigns to increase the number of visitors from districts with a large number of residents with a foreign background, for instance Eid al-Fitr is celebrated every year at the World Culture Museum.

Supporting civil society initiatives

Historically, civil society organisations and NGOs play a crucial role in organising activities and offering key services, easing integration of migrants in Gothenburg. Some NGOs (i.e. Save the Children, the Red Cross, Individuell Människohjälp, Caritas, etc.) have a long-standing presence in the most exposed areas providing services such as language classes (i.e. provided by Caritas Hjallbo in Angered for over twenty years), private coaching and tuition for school children (OECD interviews with civil society representatives, 15 March 2017). Over time, these actors guarantee the continuity of their services thanks to different contributions from the municipality, charities or foundations. Several sources of funding are available from the municipality (see section 2.3.2.) for civil society activities promoting inclusion and integration, particularly related to cultural and sport initiatives.

As observed in other cities analysed in this study, the 2015 peak in asylum seekers arrivals prompted new ways of cooperation between the municipality, civil society initiatives and NGOs. While it emerged from the interviews that there is no structured cooperation framework between civil society organisations and the municipality, these actors were able to closely collaborate in unprecedented ways in receiving asylum seekers in autumn 2015 who were either arriving or passing through Gothenburg. The municipality also cooperated with the Migration Agency and the police. This collaboration mechanism was quick to develop. Civil society organisations coordinated under the umbrella '*Welcome refugees*' accompanied the societal wave of empathy and implemented arrival assistance at the central station in Gothenburg, providing information about where to find food, water, medical assistance, access to wi-fi, clothes, blankets, toys for children. In the words of civil society organisations involved (Swedish Red Cross interviews with OECD, 15 March 2017), a good indication that the coordination worked is that there have been no casualties despite the large number of arrivals.

Innovative initiatives emerged from NGOs, host communities as well as from asylum seekers and refugees who started to develop solutions to meet their own needs. For instance, as result of the difficulties in living in temporary accommodation centres, a group of asylum seekers founded *The Support Group Network* at the Restad Gård[2]. This is a large accommodation centre for refugees outside the city of Vänersborg, approximately 10 kilometres from Gothenburg, in the Västra Götaland region. The main aim of the Network is to facilitate early paths towards the Swedish society for those waiting for the decision on their status or who have received protection. The network organised a number of supportive activities, where refugees support refugees and cooperate closely with a number of actors. For instance, the Network organised open seminars with the College West in Trollhättan and internships for those interested in higher education or employment in the academic sector. In particular, a partnership was institutionalised with Save the Children allowing the network to establish itself in 16 places throughout Sweden. This partnership received financial support from the Västra Götaland county. Based on the capacities and motivations of refugees and asylum seekers, this initiative is an example of how resourceful this group can be, autonomously seeking opportunities for empowerment and self-reliance (Meeting civil society 15 March 2017).

Cooperation under the peak of arrivals could benefit from the expertise of the civil society organisations in reception and integration activities, the empathy showed by civil society in acting for a common interest and the availability of funding for the NGOs involved.

Over time, beyond the immediate response and reception mechanisms, in the view of some of the NGOs participating in OECD interviews (Meeting 15 March 2017) the municipality does not have a long-term strategy to partner with NGOs with regards to integration and reception tasks in those areas where they would have an added value. In deed continuous dialogue with NGOs happens more at district level. This lack of long term strategy might be linked to the absence of a 'road-map' approach for mainstreaming equitable access to public services for migrants, with risks of reduced access (e.g. when public agencies ask migrants to show their identification card because they are not informed that this is no longer needed, etc.). The NGOs interviewed advocated for outsourcing services that are critical for migrants to non-state actors with relevant expertise. However measures that are implemented in parallel from the universal system should be limited to respond to specific needs that newcomers have and aim at 'accompanying' them towards the general services at arrival as well as at specific 'turning' points of their lives. NGOS and third sector entities are very well placed to operate these measures at local level. For instance they could be contracted for offering guides or translators, ensuring equal access to public services over time. In the view of some of the public servants from Gothenburg municipality who participated in OECD interviews, the time has come for the city to externalise some competence in this area to external operators.

Partnerships with local migrant associations

Traditionally, cooperation between the municipality and migrant organisations has been organised primarily at the level of the districts. Beside sport associations many cultural associations exist in the city and are sometimes an expression of the cultural heritage of one nationality such as Kurdish, Iraqi, Assyrian and Somali organisations.

Sport clubs and organisations at district level often have explicit goals of integration, and offer youth a space to meet regularly and a unifying purpose. However, membership in many sport clubs frequently mirrors the segregation that exists at district level. Spaces like the Angered Arena are attempts to make sport and leisure activities more accessible also for children with a foreign background who generally do not take part in organised sports or cultural activities as often as native Swedes (Göteborgs stad 2014: 75).

Ensure migrants and refugees democratic participation

This section focuses on immigrant civic engagement and what the municipality does to develop immigrants' knowledge of the local government system and participation opportunities.

Formal means of participation here encompass active and passive electoral rights, whereas informal means might include enrolment in political parties, keeping oneself informed of the news, participating in district or municipal consultative or decision making mechanisms and bodies, participating in grassroots initiatives, demonstrations, awareness raising activities, etc.

In terms of formal participation, differences in electoral turnout between those born inside and outside of Sweden have increased since the beginning of the 1990s. Voter turnout has been on the decline, overall, in Sweden; however, the drop is larger among foreign born than native born (SCB 2015: 62). In the parliamentary elections in 2014, 12% of those entitled to vote were born outside Sweden. The voter turnout was 89% among those born in Sweden, compared to 72% among those who were foreign born (SCB 2015). The turnout is, in general, lower among the segment of the population that was born in Asia, Africa or Europe outside of the EU. The shorter the time lived in Sweden the lower the likelihood that person will vote. Foreign-born women have a higher turnout than foreign-born men.

Differences in electoral turnout were observed during the local/municipal elections between neighbourhoods with high or lower concentrations of ethnic minorities. In the 2010 municipal election, 54% of the population that was entitled to vote actually did so in North Angered, whereas the corresponding figure for the Southwest areas was 89% (Göteborgs stad 2014: 103).

Although there aren't consultative mechanisms between the municipality and migrants and refugees communities, the city of Gothenburg actively encourages migrants to participate in both formal and informal ways in the political process. A municipal body, the Committee for Consumers Citizen Services, is tasked with improving democratic participation in the city. For instance, the Committee has identified three districts where inhabitants have a lower level of electoral participation and organised with civil society organisations initiatives to deepen democracy, trust and influence such as: mobile democracy buses, inhabitant's guides and dialogs with citizens.

Districts play a substantial role in encouraging residents' participation in planning of housing projects and residential areas, physical environment plans, security and leisure activities. All district councils have dialogues with their inhabitants depending on the topic via local advisory boards consisting of elderly, young or disabled. Some districts decided to set up participatory budget initiatives others decided to focus their dialogues around security, safe environments for children upbringing, or urban development. In order to encourage migrants' participation, information on different societal matters is provided by the districts in several languages, especially when substantial changes are meant to occur or are being planned. At the same time, the number of persons born abroad who have been politically appointed on boards and in decision-making organisations has increased.

With regards to asylum seekers, it emerged from interviews with representatives of the refugee Support group, that often this category feels cut off from any interaction with public authorities. They explained that there is little official communication from the government to asylum seekers throughout the decision on their status. For those who live in camps in isolated areas the extended time period they must go without communication can have consequences on their attitude to participate as active citizens in their new society once their claims are accepted.

Migration perception and Communication with citizens

The Swedish population is divided on issues related to migration and immigration, and the debate is heated in politics and in the media, like in many other countries. Immigration and integration have become contested and polarised issues, and according to longitudinal studies on opinions and attitudes immigration was *the* most important issue for the Swedish population in 2015 (Ohlsson, Oscarsson och Solevid 2016: 14). As previously stated, the large influx of refugees in 2015 caused a wave of empathy and large sectors of the civil society mobilised to provide assistance and organise demonstrations and marches under the banner *Welcome Refugees*. The Swedish population is generally accepting of refugees and only 40% of the Swedish population in 2015 said Sweden should receive fewer refugees, the lowest figure since 1990 (Demker & van der Meiden 2016). In 2016, there was, however, a sharp rise in this number, to 52% (SOM 2017). In parallel, there has also been an increase in attitudes of rejection of foreigners in Swedish society. This trend started since the 1990s, when so-called White Power mobilisation resulted in greater visibility for racist organisations and political groups, and took a sharp turn from 2010, with the rise of the Sweden Democrats. This is now the third largest party in the parliament (*Riksdagen)* with 13% of the votes in the parliamentary elections in 2014. In the local elections in Gothenburg in 2014, the Sweden Democrats received 7%. Different studies observed an increase in Sweden of violence against minorities (BRÅ 2016; Expo 2016, SVT 2017).

Further, the perception that criminality and violence are related to suburban areas, characterised by a high presence of ethnic minorities, increases tendencies of segregation and divisions as certain areas are then called, in the public discourse, dangerous 'no-go zones' (Forkby & Hansson 2011: 15). Statistics show that there is a certain overrepresentation in crime among people born outside of Sweden, but when this is correlated to socio-economic conditions, differences between Swedish born and foreign born almost disappear (Forkby & Hansson 2011: 60). The perception around the link between violence and ethnic minorities has been exacerbated in recent years by more spectacular modes of protest or violent behaviour among youth groups and gangs in Gothenburg suburb areas.

Against this backdrop, the municipality established specific joint programmes with the police to make the presence of the institutions more tangible in exposed areas as well as organising communication and information activities.

Box 3.2. Police and municipality joint project in exposed areas

In 2016, the Gothenburg municipality and the police launched the project "Safe in Gothenburg". The municipality and the police cooperate to increase trust between residents and representatives of public institutions in exposed areas, reduce segregation and increase the areas' attractiveness. The projects adopt a bottom-up approach: the residents define their most pressing security problems in the neighbourhood and the police address them through targeted activities in collaboration with the city's social workers (Meeting with the Police, 16 March 2017). While building a common problem statement, the police establishes a space of confidence where residents can express their issues related to crime and safety. For instance, in Angered, residents considered littering and annoying traffic in the form of mopeds and motorcycles as problematic. The municipality and the police considered low school results, unemployment, criminality among youth, organised criminality and sales of drugs as issues to be addressed. All of those issues were then collected in a joint action plan. A municipal police officer is in charge of implementing the action plan, coordinating between the society, the municipality and the police so crime drops and residents feel safer.

During the peak in refugee and asylum seeker arrivals, the municipality dealt with negative attitudes and fears related to establishing accommodations for unaccompanied minors or adult refugees by holding information meetings in order to answer the concerns raised by residents (Meeting Gothenburg municipality, 16 March 2017). Accordingly, NGOs noticed that there was more resistance to activities for assisting refugees in neighbourhoods with fewer foreign-born residents rather than in the more diverse ones and that in rural areas the residents sometimes were willing to keep refugees who lived in the camps once they were closed (OECD interviews with CSOs 15 March 2017). In general, the municipality does not systematically react to the results of opinion polls on immigration; it tends to continue to implement its policies (Additional information provided by the City Executive Office, 9 May 2017).

More informal mechanisms influencing attitudes and public opinion have been set up by the civil society with new organisations engaging in creating positive attitudes and opinions vis-à-vis newcomers. Examples are Together for Gothenburg[3] (*Tillsammans för Göteborg*), Agape's activities for unaccompanied minors, Stop the Expulsions of Afghan youth (*Stoppa utvisningarna av afghanska ungdomar*) #wecan'tstandit (*#vistårinteut)*[4], working to change the situation of unaccompanied minors, anti-racism campaigns initiated by the Swedish Red Cross. Many of these new initiatives are loosely organised, sometimes spontaneous. By using social media/Facebook they contribute to creating a positive attitude towards migrants and to mobilising different publics around various events. It has been observed by civil society organisations (CSOs) that through volunteer activities Swedish people can experience the advantages of having a diverse society (OECD interviews with CSOs 15 March 2017).

Notes

[1] http://goteborg.se/wps/portal/start/kommun-o-politik/kommunens-organisation/forvaltningar/forvaltningar/social-resursforvaltning/vara-verksamheter/integrationscentrum-goteborg

[2] http://supportgroup.se/index.html

[3] An organisation which exists in many cities throughout Sweden, under the umbrella ''Together for…''

[4] Initiated by professionals in health care, teachers and social workers.

Chapter 4. Block 3. Enabling conditions

Objective 6: Build-up capacity and diversity in civil service, particularly in the key services that receive migrants and newcomers

Among the 30 proposals that the city drafted to reduce inequality (Gothenburg, 2014[3]) many deal with the capacity development of the City itself, particularly in terms of capacity to interact, and establish public dialogue around inequality issues. Improving the knowledge of public servants about the rights and status of migrants is one of the priorities highlighted by civil society organisations. For instance, NGOs felt that rights-based access could sometimes be problematic due to the lack of knowledge about migrants' status of public services (see section 2.2.2).

Objective 7: Strengthen cooperation with relevant stakeholders through transparent and effective contracts

According to information collected during the focus group held by the OECD with several NGOs operating in Gothenburg (15 March 2017) there is no structured cooperation framework with associations involved in receiving new arrivals, but it is something that the city wants to develop and the Central Management group is tasked with this issue (see section 2.1.2.4.).

In general, civil society organisations can apply for several municipal funds for integration-related activities through different departments and local districts. For instance, the boards in charge of culture and sport offer support for groups that organise cultural and sport activities respectively. Migrant organisations are often funded through local districts.

The Committee for allocation of social welfare, responsible for issues related to social affairs, manages a fund for activities related to social welfare, and disability that all NGOs can apply for. However there is no specific call for application for integration projects The fund is geared towards NGOs working in the following priority areas: supporting people in need of support based on their social situation, on social violence, oppression; increasing participation in social affairs; promoting public health; supporting disabled people, creating jobs for people in social distress, etc., (Additional information provided by the City Executive Office, 23 May 2017).

Furthermore, the Social Resource Management Board is responsible for a structured cooperation model with NGOs, named *IDÉKOM*. This is a platform for exchanging ideas between the municipality and representatives of what is labelled the "social economy", composed of non-governmental organisations and private sector entities working in the municipality on socioeconomic issues, including migration.

Another type of structured and long-term cooperation is "Ideational Public Partnership" (IOP). This is a public-volunteer partnership between non for profit entities (i.e. NGOs) and public services (i.e. municipalities). According to NGOs interviewed (OECD interviews 15 March 2017) this model of partnership allows municipalities to sign umbrella agreements with NGOs avoiding a lengthy procurement process and choosing more flexibly the partners it wants to work with. Under this umbrella agreement, specific agreements can be made for occasional activities. For example, the agreements between the municipality and associations delivering accommodation for unaccompanied minors were signed using an IOP. Those agreements were made in 2016 and run until 2019. Also with regard to activities related to labour market integration, the Labour and Adult Education Administration recently started to co-operate with NGOs using the Ideational Public Partnership format, to implement long-term projects to support vulnerable groups entering the labour market (Additional information provided by the City Executive Office, 23 May 2017). Another example of an IOP partnership is the agreement between SOS Children's villages and the municipality that focuses on ways to empower unaccompanied refugee children, between 15 and 21 years of age.

Despite the existence of such umbrella agreements, NGOs participating in OECD interviews, reported being penalised by segmented funding mechanisms that target migrant groups. Funding is often disbursed by different municipal agencies/departments, undermining the ability of NGOs to support migrants throughout their lives as they obtain funding for very specific categories of beneficiaries. Additionally, in the view of some NGOs, outsourcing some services such as psychological support or language classes to third parties would generate efficiency gains as some of these services are more expensive when provided by the municipality than by NGOs. While the funding from municipal authorities is provided for specific periods and groups, NGOs are still able to provide services over time and maintain their expertise due to other un-earmarked financial resources (e.g. charities, faith-based funding, etc.) that allow them to continue providing services to all vulnerable groups.

Also the region of Vastra Gotaland can provide funding for activities in the area of integration directly to NGOs and refugee organisations. For instance, the region funded the Support Group (see section 2.2.2.) first through Save the Children and then directly.

Objective 8: Intensify assessment of integration results for migrants and host communities, and their use for evidence-based policy making

The governmental agency Statistics Sweden (SBC) compiles and publishes statistical data used for monitoring integration (UNHCR, 2014). Statistics focus on individuals born outside Sweden and those with parents born outside. This statistic does not distinguish for refugees. Statistical data related to several indicators are presented by geographic origin, gender and age, and can be analysed at the national, regional and municipal level, including urban areas identified as having widespread socio-economic exclusion.

STATIV is another database produced by SCB and records immigration status and includes reasons for immigration; therefore, it can be useful to track refugees. Moreover, the Ministry of Employment conducts quantitative analysis and qualitative studies to assess different integration areas, also this statistic does not distinguish for refugees.

All County Administrative Boards have prepared, since 2012, an annual report[1] on the settlement and introduction programmes for newly arrived refugees. The report is based on a survey to all municipalities in the county, and contains questions about the local and regional co-operation and co-ordination, capacity and willingness to receive new arrivals and unaccompanied children, and the quality of reception and introduction activities.

The city of Gothenburg established systems that monitor inequalities in living conditions and health between different groups and different districts in the city. Among the proposals for reducing inequality in Gothenburg, the city wants to strengthen its capacity in terms of operational evaluation, facilitating analysis and measurement (Gothenburg, 2014[3]). Particularly, the city aims to measure the consequences of inequality, in terms of health and living conditions, in order to take them into account in the organisation's existing analysis and follow up system. At the moment, no system is in place to monitor specifically the integration outcomes of new migrants or refugees in the city. According to the municipality however, evaluations on different aspects relevant to integration are made continuously. One example is the fact that newly arrived adults receive information and societal orientation in their mother tongue, which is the result of previous evaluations and experiences. (Additional information provided by the City Executive Office, 9 May 2017).

Note

[1] http://www.lansstyrelsen.se/jonkoping/SiteCollectionDocuments/Sv/publikationer/2017/2017-16-Mottagande-och-etablering-av-nyanlanda.pdf

Chapter 5. Block 4. Sectoral Measures

Objective 9: Match migrant skills with economic and job opportunities

Context: Improvements and persistent gaps in migrants' access to the labour market

The Swedish economy is growing rapidly with new opportunities arising all the time (OECD, 2017a[23]). In March 2017, it was reported that 244 000 new jobs had been created between 2008 and 2016. Most of those jobs went to foreign-born individuals, due to the demographic structures in Sweden, where native born in their productive years do not meet demands of labour in a growing and expanding economy (SvT 2017b). However, recent reports are somewhat contradictory with regards to access to the job market for persons with a foreign background. On the one hand, they confirm the division of the Swedish labour market (Arbetsmarknadsekonomiska rådet 2017) only 35% of the migrant population are full-time employed in permanent positions, compared to 61% of Swedish born. In 2016, 33.3% of foreign born on the labour market considered themselves to be overqualified in relation to the position they held, as compared to 17.3% for native born Swedes (SCB 2016). On the other hand, a trend indicates that the level of employment is increasing among those with a foreign background (SCB 2017).

In recent decades, it has been more difficult for refugees arriving in Sweden to find a place in the labour market (Arbetsekonomiska rådet 2017: 13), and the employment population ratio among newly-arrived refugees and their families dropped to around 8% in Sweden. However, there are differences in this ratio across the country and the extent to which these migrants move into employment in their first 7-10 years in Sweden. In Vastra Gotaland, for instance, there is a 30 percentage point difference between the ratio of employed refugee population of those living in Sweden for 0-2 years and those who have lived in Sweden for 7-10 years. In other provinces, this difference is only 20 points (Skane) whereas in the most high-performing ones the difference across years reaches approximately 43 points difference. The local autonomy in education policy design and implementation is largely behind this success (OECD, 2016[11]).

Opportunities to move into the job market are related also to the skills and competence of newcomers as low-skilled professions have been decreasing in Sweden in line with a strong digitalisation trend. Recruiters require applicants to have completed at least an upper-secondary school, leaving very little jobs for those who have no or pre-secondary education (Arbetsförmedlingen, 2017). However, the Chamber of Commerce in Gothenburg (OECD interviews 15 March 2017) reported that given the high labour demand some employers (i.e. engineering, etc.) have started lowering their expectations in terms of language skills and accepts applications from English speakers as long as they meet the technical requirements.

It should also be noted, that there is a fairly high proportion of self-employed and small business establishment among the foreign-born, especially among men born in Middle

Eastern countries (Arbetsmarknadsekonomiska rådet 2017). For instance in 2012, 4.8% of Swedish-born men were self-employed; 7.7% of men born in Iran; 11.4% of men born in Syria, and 1.0% of men born in Somalia (Aldén & Hammarstedt 2017).

At regional level, according to the 2016 Report published by the Swedish Public employment service (PES) in the Vastra Gotalands region (Arbetsförmedlingen, 2017), the situation is similar to the national picture. Employment is increasing and there are good opportunities for new entry in the job market. However there is a risk of double polarisation. Geographic labour market polarisation: due to urbanisation and demographic transition causing depopulation in some areas. And a polarisation around most vulnerable groups in the labour market: unemployed with only pre-secondary education, born outside Europe, aged 55-64 years, reduced work skills. In this region, labour shortages are expected in both the short and long term in the following sectors: health services, teachers, engineers and IT, construction and civil engineers, qualified professions in industry, etc. (OECD meeting with Arbetsförmedlingen 16 March 2017).

In the city of Gothenburg, labour market segregation is among the top three most pressing challenges for the municipality. The gap in employment ratio for foreign background and Swedish background population is 22 percentage points. 76.1% of the population were employed in 2014 in Gothenburg. 84.3% of those with a Swedish background had a job, compared to 61.2% of those with a foreign background (see table 7.1). 6.2% of the population of Gothenburg were unemployed in 2014 (see table 7.2); 3.6% of those with a Swedish background and 12.6% of those with a foreign background. The gaps are higher when considering areas in the city characterised by higher presence of persons with a foreign background, reaching 53.9 % in the neighbourhoods with a higher percentage of migrant population such as Angered. Long-time unemployed are overrepresented in areas such as Bergsjön and South Angered (Gothenburg, 2014[3]).

Table 5.1. Employment rate per district

District	Employment rate	
	Foreign born	Swedish born
Angered	53.9	76.3
Östra Göteborg	52.6	77.2
Örgryte/Härlanda	66.7	86.4
Centrum	64.1	83.5
Majorna/Linné	67.8	83.7
Askim/Frölunda/Högsbo	64.1	84.6
Västra Göteborg	66.1	87.6
Västra Hisingen	59.6	86.8
Lundby	68.4	84.6
Norra Hisingen	68.5	86
Göteborg as a whole	61.2	84.3

Source: Göteborgsbladet 2016.

Table 5.2. Unemployment rate per district in Gothenburg

District	Unemployment rate	
	Foreign born	Swedish born
Angered	16.1	7.3
Östra Göteborg	17.5	5.2
Örgryte/Härlanda	9.6	2.9
Centrum	6.6	2.7
Majorna/Linné	8.3	3.7
Askim/Frölunda/Högsbo	10.2	3.5
Västra Göteborg	11.6	2.8
Västra Hisingen	14.8	3.5
Lundby	9.7	3.5
Norra Hisingen	10.7	3.6
Göteborg as a whole	12.6	3.6

Source: Göteborgsbladet 2016

In Gothenburg, foreign-born workers find employment mainly in the following sectors: construction, health and medical care, whole and retail trade, repair of motor vehicles, transportation and storage, hotel and restaurants and food service activities as well as in the education sector (OECD Questionnaire completed by the city of Gothenburg for this study, 2017).

With respect to refugee integration in the labour market, in Gothenburg only 20% of those who completed the introduction programme continue to study or work after the two years. The municipality is concerned about the long waiting time before recognised status holders can work and they plead for more efficient early measures for newly arrived individuals (OECD meeting with the municipality 16 March 2017).

Labour market policies

The Swedish government is focusing on ''employability'', in its current refugee integration efforts and the key instrument is the Introduction programme[1] introduced in 2010[2]. The objective of this integration model is to get status holders into jobs, education or training within two years[3]. After two years, if the person is not within any of those activities, there are no special measures, but the individual is entitled to the same social support as anyone else in Sweden, for a full description of the activities and benefits available to the unemployed and the social assistance payments see (OECD, 2016[11])

In Gothenburg, as in the rest of Sweden the PES office[4] is responsible for all introduction activities for newly arrived adults whilst the municipalities are responsible for providing Swedish language courses for immigrants (SFI), housing, initiatives for children in schools and pre-school as well as civic orientation services (Bakbasel, 2012). National accreditation agencies are tasked with validating their educational and professional experience.

Relevant considerations for fostering refugees' integration in the labour market at local level

The following key findings relate to the implementation of the introduction programme and as well as to other local activities

- Refugees' skill assessment could be improved across levels. The first step towards making refugees employable is assessing and evaluating previous knowledge, expertise and education (Diedrich & Styhre, 2015). A competence mapping is undertaken by the Migration board in an early stage of the asylum seeking process. However, the PES tends to begin its own evaluation during the first introduction meeting with refugees who received a residence permit. Municipalities often consider they do not enough information on migrants' past education and experience and therefore often repeat the mapping exercise before allocating newcomers to language classes (OECD, 2016[11]). The support granted while applicants' status is pending is limited to basic language training, but as noted in previous OECD work, these activities could be strengthened and tracked in a centralised database to which municipalities and government agencies have access in order to build upon previous investments.

- Local coordination when identifying introduction activities could be improved. During one or more introduction interviews[5] at the local PES office, a personalised introduction plan is drawn up. Based on the person's experience, education, interests and ambitions this plan will determine which complementary education and activities, such as internships with employers, the person will be oriented towards. In this exercise, the municipality could be more involved, so as to connect very early PES's tools with municipal offers of vocational training and local capacity to match profiles and offers.

- Local Offer of vocational training: As observed in previous OECD work (OECD, 2016[11]) education courses provided to refugee job seekers at the same time by the PES and the municipality can result in duplication, and loss in efficiency, which could be avoided through better coordination. Municipalities have experience in training social welfare claimants who are far removed from the labour market[6], while the PES training offered to refugees during the first two years might not be sufficiently intensive for those who need remedial education in preparation for the labour market. Often, municipalities develop labour market training, targeting established humanitarian migrants claiming social assistance, who no longer have access to the introduction programme. If the municipality was involved since the first interviews with recognised refugees, alongside PES caseworkers in the PES district offices, they could jointly assess the needs and orient those refugees who will have the hardest time finding work towards the most appropriate municipal programmes. Other cities avoid this overlap by establishing one-stop-shops for newcomers (i.e. Start Wien office) where refugees' skills and aspirations are assessed, and they can be oriented towards courses offered by all relevant actors: employment or welfare services or private education. In Amsterdam, the municipality offers tailored support to newcomers through case managers, like in Sweden, but it then directly contracts (private or public) suppliers to assess newcomers' skills and strengthen their capacities through education or vocational courses.

- Links with the private sector at city level: It emerged from interviews with the private sector in Gothenburg that the Introduction programme could benefit from improving its links with the local private sector (OECD meetings 16 March 2017). The PES could improve the information accessible to local businesses with regards to newcomers' competences and strengthen the collaboration with the local branch of the Swedish Chamber of Commerce. As an example, recently a company from the region reported that it published an advertisement for 60 positions and managed to identify enough refugee candidates who match the requirements. Unfortunately, only four of them could be hired due to bureaucratic obstacles associated with their permits or the distance from the municipality where their residence had been assigned. The Employment agency recognised that due to the high amount of newcomers they could not keep up the quality of the database and regularly share the information on the existing profiles. They are working on this as well as on improving their screening tool. These findings are in line with previous OECD research: while the PES is particularly important for migrants as a job-research method, employers reduced the number of vacancies they notify to the PES database and are reluctant to use the PES to source their candidates as they feel it is unable to identify the requested professional and educational background and lack sufficient industry knowledge (OECD, 2016[11]). During interviews with the OECD (Meeting City executive council officers, 16 March 2017) the municipality also noted a need for increased cooperation with the private sector. For instance, there seems to be little information on the private sector side about the incentives programme implemented by the Employment services, which pay 80% of an individual's salary for a period of time to businesses that hire migrants. There has been little evidence of the uptake of this opportunity by businesses in Gothenburg, as well as in other Swedish regions such as Småland Blekinge

- Sensitize employers to recruiting employees: some municipal companies such as the city's housing company, has initiated measures to increase refugees' access to the jobs, in cooperation with the employment service. For instance, they offer refugees Swedish classes and an internship within the housing group as well as with subcontractors such as cleaning companies and construction companies.

A study on the effects of the Introduction Act shows small, but significant positive effects on both levels of employment and wage level among the foreign-born. Two years after participating in the Introduction programme, the level of employment was 5.7% higher for those who had taken part in the reform programme than for those who had not. Three years afterwards, the corresponding figure was 7.5%. (Andersson, Joona, Wennemo Lanninger & Sundström 2016).

An overall consideration emerged from interviews with different stakeholders, levels of employment among refugees might increase more quickly if the support would start earlier. As mentioned above, the average time for completion of the settlement process was 239 days, *before* refugee could access the Introduction activities.

Beyond the introduction programme some important initiatives are implemented by Business Region Gothenburg, which is an agency responsible for business development in the City of Gothenburg and represents thirteen municipalities in the region.[7] Business region implements in partnership with other actors (i.e. city districts, city departments, the Swedish Red Cross, Sahlgrenska Academy of the university of Gothenburg etc.) projects focusing on newcomers who have experience in trading or entrepreneurship. For instance they guide people who have a business concept to get it started through counselling, financing and support.

Another very interesting matching experience is the one implemented between 2015-2016 by the Göteborg Region Association of Local Authorities (GR). 8 municipalities in the Gothenburg region participated in the project together with the regional company Gryaab, to match employers' recruitment needs with the engineering skills of newcomers. After the success of the pilot in 2016-2017 the country administrative board funded a new project - På rätt plats8- involving 10 employers, government agencies, municipalities, union and trade associations (Aarsleff, Gothenburg City, Gryaab, Kungsbacka municipality, Lerum municipality, Mölndal municipality, Älvstranden Utveckling and WSP). The project proves that internships were effective for enter the labour market (14 employment out of 14 trainees). The project has also revealed that employers' ability to introduce and supervise the interns is very important for a successful integration in the workplace.

Objective 10: Secure access to adequate housing

A general shortage of housing in the larger cities of Sweden constitutes a bottleneck for refugee accommodation, as well as for young adults moving out from parental homes and for international recruitment of labour force and students. This is due to the fact that in Sweden, construction of housing has not kept up with population increases. Deciding what should be built and where is a municipal responsibility, which partially explains the uneven distribution of housing construction and permit requirements across the country. In addition, the planning process for new housing can take up to three years (OECD, 2016[11]).

Municipal housing companies, which represent a significant share of all rental accommodation in Sweden, manage public housing (i.e. apartments for private rent at reasonable prices). Everybody in Sweden is supposed to cover the rent themselves – no social housing – but there are options to apply for assistance to defray housing costs.

In Gothenburg, the housing shortage worsened markedly in the autumn of 2015 by the arrivals of large numbers of refugees and asylum seekers. However, this was not a new trend. According to the 2016 Gothenburg Economic Outlook (Business Region Goteborg, 2016) housing prices in the city and in the metropolitan region have increased since 2012 - by 9% over one year in 2016. In fact, the Outlook estimates that the shortage of homes and increasing demand, due to significant inward migration, in combination with low mortgage rates that increase real estate demand, will continue to drive prices up in the region for some years. In addition, contained prices in the public housing, and limited new construction led to extreme rental housing shortages and very high rents in the private housing market.

Housing responsibility in the city of Gothenburg

The municipal real estate committee is responsible for the land and housing policy of the City of Gothenburg.

The Real Estate board of the city of Gothenburg creates the conditions for building new housing: identifying land and exploitation; buying, selling and leasing of land; management of land and buildings. Many municipalities, including Gothenburg, have substantial land holdings that give them an important tool to shape land use in their territory either by choosing directly how to build the land they own or by deciding to sell it to private developers (OECD, 2017[17]). In view of ensuring city sustainability the Property Management committee requires that tenants, who hold the rights to build new housing, ensure that a certain proportion will have low rents.

Access to housing for vulnerable groups in Gothenburg

Compared to other Swedish cities, Gothenburg is an exception as public housing companies still owns 30% of the housing stock whereas other cities have sold their housing stock to private companies. There are four public housing companies in

Gothenburg, all sorted under The Future Concern (Förvaltnings AB Framtiden): a real estate company owned by the municipality, dealing with housing, property management and building of new housing. The public housing companies offer housing for everyone. Rents are collectively negotiated, which keep them lower than the marginal market price. In 2016, there were 40 vacant apartments in the Gothenburg public housing stock, out of a total of 72 338, representing a vacancy level of 0.1%. Those who received a contract in 2016 had had to queue for an average time of 1 606 days (4.4 years) until signing the contract. The city has a cooperation agreement with both the city's housing companies and private housing companies to free a quota of apartments for people who need help with housing for social or medical reasons. The agreement is revised annually. The public housing companies in Gothenburg have themselves decided to set aside a number of apartments for vulnerable groups including people with disabilities, homeless and refugees. In 2014, the city decided on a special venture with the housing company for families with children including new arrivals who had particularly difficult housing conditions.

Housing for refugees

As explained in chapter 4.3 asylum seekers' accommodation is a national responsibility. However, according to the 2016 Settlements Act, housing of those who received a positive response to their asylum seeking application and requested assistance for accommodation, is a responsibility of the municipality where they have been assigned by the Migration agency.

During two years, refugees who participate in the Introduction programme receive housing allowance to be spent on the public or private market. After that time, refugees might receive housing compensation as part of other programmes for labour market participation or as social benefits like all other citizens. There is nothing automatic in the system, but applications are evaluated and judged in accordance with level of income and capacity to provide for oneself and one's family. Particular attention is given to people between 18-24 and families with children registered as living in the county. These allocations are provided through the municipality social security system, and are financed by taxes. For those who live as hidden refugees or who are undocumented, there are no such possibilities.

In 2015, 2 300 refugees were referred to Gothenburg through the national mechanism and 1100 in 2017. Unaccompanied minors were 1 700 in 2015, as compared to 400 in 2014. Housing has been provided for all of them. At the same time, there were 3 000-4 000 new asylum seekers in accommodation organised by the Migration Agency or refugees and asylum seekers who individually arranged their accommodation in the city. In 2017, the municipality estimated that just 40% of status-holders benefitted from accommodation provided by the municipality as the majority found their own housing solutions. As described in Chapter 4.3, the possibility for humanitarian migrants to find individually arranged accommodation is a matter of strong debate in Sweden for its consequences in terms of concentration of large numbers of migrants in specific areas, potentially leading to overcrowded housing, segregation and social exclusion problems (Joyce, 2017).

While the Establishment Unit provides support with bureaucratic procedures to access housing, the Property Management Administration and the Real estate committee of the municipality of Gothenburg had to find solutions for sub-letting apartments for four years to refugees assigned through the national mechanism. After 4 years, the apartment returns to the open system and the tenant must find housing by her/his own means

(Meeting The Future Concern 16 March 2017). Discussion is ongoing in the municipality to foresee what assistance is still needed to find a permanent residence after the four years. The City's housing company Förvaltnings AB Framtiden has a commitment to provide apartments to newly arrived refugees. In 2017 they rented 450 apartments to refugees. 80 apartments in 2017 were provided by privately owned housing companies[9]. Currently, there are 500 apartments in the stock for newcomers. Housing companies had to change their regulation that previously required all tenants to have a minimum income in order to make refugees eligible.

The priority given to refugee to available houses is imposed by the new law that obliges municipalities to provide housing to assigned newcomers. However it has been debated how the allocation of apartments to immigrants affects other groups that are in need of housing as well as the specific need of this group and the fact that other solutions i.e. hostels, hotels will be more costly and far from optimal in terms of integration perspective especially for children. In the words of Gothenburg officials (Meeting Property Management Administration 14 March 2018) this law gives an opportunity and an obligation to the city to control where newcomers are offered housing solutions. So far this had the effect of avoiding concentrating newcomers in neighbourhood which are already segregated and disperse them equally across the city.

In fact, the city had been looking for housing solutions for receiving refugees for some years. In 2014, a strategy for housing of newly-arrived refugees was adopted by the municipal government in order to meet short-term needs (Förslag till strategi för bostadsförsörjning för nyanlända). In partnership with Future Concern, the municipality decided that temporary housing was to be built in Frihamnen for newly arrived, but also for students and apartments to be used by companies. Roughly a third of the stock was to be rented by the municipality, which would in turn rent them out to newly arrived individuals. Those plans have now been scuttled as the project appears to be more expensive than planned and as the building permit has not yet been cleared (GP 2017).

Long-term solutions to increase availability and affordability of housing in Gothenburg

In line with its growing population (4 400 new residents in 2016), Gothenburg's plans for new construction are ambitious in volume and in scope: 80 000 new housing units are planned until 2035. Sustainability is a leading principle in new strategies of urban planning and social aspects are integrated. One of the main projects is located in Älvstranden in the area of formal industrial sites connected to the shipyard industry. Urban planning is concentrated in such areas where the municipality owns the land. These development projects represent clear attempts to combat segregation through creating attractive and affordable housing environments where heterogeneous groups would like to live.

National incentives for creating affordable housing are limited. The municipality incentivizes developers involved in new projects to provide suggestions for how to create a more socially sustainable housing situation. The Future Concern Group, a consortium of public housing companies, is in charge of developing this project. New development projects are financed according to financial regulations established by the municipality. The funding of public housing companies originates partly from rents, partly by return from an increase in value in the public housing stock and partly from credits from the private financial market. In these areas, there will be a mix of apartments for rent and family-owned houses. The dilemma is how to maintain low costs in new urban housing areas to make them affordable to various swaths of the population.

By building these new areas, the demand for labour and construction workers will increase, creating jobs for newly arrived. As one representative of the public housing companies said: ''We now have an opportunity to heal the city'', through building in an inclusive way, while at the same time creating job opportunities for newly arrived (OECD Meeting with public housing companies 16 March 2017).

Objective 11: Provide social welfare measures that are aligned with migrant inclusion

Social welfare

Social assistance in Sweden is allocated by municipalities. Social services are managed by the Social resource management and funded by the state through taxes. This service provides support to the social service office of each district in Gothenburg. Within this service, a specific unit called the Establishment unit (*Etableringsenheten*) provides support for newly arrived enrolled in the Introduction programme, but also for relatives and for unaccompanied minors. The unit offers support and information to those groups with regards to a number of social services: administers their applications for economic assistance, orient them to health suppliers and rehabilitation services and provides information for instance on child support, schooling and preschool (Meeting with Establishment unit 16 March 2017). The existence of a municipal unit intending to help persons in the Introduction programme in finding their way in the system is specific to Gothenburg.

As stated before, the general principle is that everyone, including refugees, should provide for her/himself, so social assistance is only allocated in case their income is insufficient. During the Introduction programme, refugees receive, through the municipality, remuneration from Social Insurance, intended to cover costs of food and other necessities. The remuneration amounts to SEK 308 per day, five days a week, which totals 6 160 SEK per month (€630). There is an additional contribution that can be provided for those who have children, and there are possibilities of receiving assistance for housing costs (see housing section above).

At the end of the introduction programme, refugees will receive the same treatment as every resident who is eligible for social services based on his/her income. Refugees rarely qualify for unemployment compensation because they have rarely worked in Sweden long enough, therefore they largely rely on social assistance, which depends on municipalities as well as housing allocations that are provided through the municipality social security system, and are financed by taxes. EU migrants (EU/EEA-citizens) who are not economically active (seeking employment) only have the right to certain basic/emergency support mechanisms, provided by the municipal social services. If economically active, citizens of EU member states are entitled to social welfare benefits on the same basis as Swedish citizens. Vulnerable EU migrants often lack access to housing, and rely on the support of voluntary organisations and faith-based activities, that offer a number of night shelters.

Health care

Health and medical care is organised by the county council for the Västra Götaland region (VGR). All publicly-funded health care institutions in Sweden offer free health care to everybody who is registered in Sweden and has a social security number.

Access to health care for EU/EEA citizens is unclearly defined and their treatment varies from county to county in Sweden (Dagens Medicin 2016). For EU citizens who live in Sweden but do not plan to apply for healthcare service in Sweden they need to obtain a prior authorisation from that Swedish Social Insurance Agency (Försäkringskassan) and show that the home country is responsible for healthcare costs other than emergency care[10].

Primary care or local health centres offer free medical examination of refugees. This has been offered since 2012 and includes screening for trauma and human rights abuses as well as other medical problems.

Asylum seekers have a right to health care that cannot be deferred, i.e. maternity care, health examination and dental care. They have the right to translation services, free of charge if they do not understand Swedish. Since 2013, undocumented migrants as well as hidden refugees have the right to subsidised health care to the same extent as asylum seekers[11]. All children up to the age of 18 have the right to full care, as well as dental care, on the same terms as all other children living in the county council where they are seeking treatment.

''Health in Sweden 2017-2018'' is a new project within the Västra Götaland region aiming at promoting health for asylum seekers. A main priority is to provide information to refugees about the health system and to work closely with civil society actors in the field of health (OECD Meeting with Health in Sweden 16 March, 2017). In 2017, SEK 10 million were allocated to this project and further financing is planned for 2018, an evaluation took place in autumn 2017 (Information by the Västra Götaland region 22 May 2017).

Some health services in Gothenburg provide tailored assistance for the specific needs of certain refugees and migrants. The Trauma and Crisis Clinic in Gothenburg offers specialised therapy and treatment for trauma caused by the effects of war and torture. In 2016, the clinic was visited by 2 000 individuals and had 300 referrals for crisis and trauma (Meeting with the Trauma and Crisis Clinic, 16 March, 2017). In 2015, the Angered Public Hospital was inaugurated by the regional authority. The purpose of localising a hospital in Angered was to bring health care closer to the inhabitants of this district characterised by a large presence of inhabitants with a migration background. The hospital is specialised in paediatric and child psychiatric services. Furthermore, within the large Sahlgrenska University Hospital, there has been, since 2007, a special team focusing on refugee children, The Child Refugee Team which appears to be a unique feature of health in Gothenburg. The team uses an integrated approach and works also to support other functions of society in helping refugee children.

NGOs operating in the health sector play an important role in Gothenburg. They had an important role for instance in access to healthcare for undocumented migrants, influencing lawmakers and politicians. NGOs collect information on groups that are still excluded from access to health care and try to influence the politicians to change their situation. A good example is Rosengenska, a Gothenburg-based NGO created in 1998 that counts on 200 volunteer health care professionals, doctors and nurses. The NGOs operate in the most vulnerable areas of the city, providing care for undocumented migrants and hidden refugees. Their work is driven from a rights-based perspective and receives funding from the "Ideational Public Partnership" (IOP) and voluntary sources.

Objective 12: Establish education responses to address segregation and provide equitable paths to professional growth

Sweden's education system is among the most decentralised in OECD countries. Municipalities on the local level have autonomy in designing policies and practices, which therefore vary to a great extent throughout the country and across schools (OECD 2010: 8). According to OECD recent analysis, although the municipalisation reform started 20 years ago the perception of responsibility is still not entirely clearly defined between the national and municipal level and within municipalities themselves: "municipalisation of schooling has shifted many responsibilities to municipalities without accompanying this shift with corresponding support for capacity building or necessary human and financial resources" (Blanchenay, Burns and Köster, 2014[24]).

Municipalities are in charge of primary and secondary schools. In Sweden, there is a strong tradition of independent learning institutions, providing education in a number of fields to all groups in society. Independent schools are outside of the municipal system although Swedish legislation stipulates that the municipalities are to allocate grants to the independent schools according to the same principles the municipality use when distributing funds to its own schools (Education, 2016[25]). Independent schools are obliged adhere to national curriculum and upper secondary programme objectives. The difference is limited to the subjects the schools offer: independent schools tend to have more specialised profiles whereas public schools usually cater to either arts or sports interests (Blanchenay, Burns and Köster, 2014[24]). Independent schools are mostly structured as a collection of small-scale providers and large-scale school companies with multiple sites (OECD, 2015[26]). In this context, where funding is largely dependent on municipal budgets, education and professional development strategies as well as policies for students with a migration background largely depend on local rather than national prerogatives (OECD, 2015[26]).

Given the clear understanding that municipalities have of the size and composition of their student population, local policies can more strategically address education gaps. For instance, previous OECD work (OECD, OECD Reviews of migrant education. Sweden, 2010) highlighted the role of municipalities in building capacities of school staff to meet the specific needs of immigrant students and their parents. In particular, it recommended that teacher education and training include priority components such as formative assessment, action-research, second language acquisition, and intercultural education. Through such universal measures, not only immigrant students but also native students will benefit. However, recent evidence (OECD, 2015[26])clearly shows wide variations across municipal capacity to provide the kind of recruitment, induction, mentoring, and continuing professional development necessary to support sustained improvements in teaching. Thus, efforts are needed to have a strong focus on monitoring and evaluation of professional development programmes at national level to reduce inequalities in the quality of the education profession.

Gaps in educational outcomes and attainment

Overall, migrant children in Sweden have lower educational outcomes compared to their native peers, while the largest disparities between the two groups are more visible in upper secondary education. However, in line with the results of The Swedish National

Agency for Education (*Skolverket*) reports, OECD research (OECD 2010) suggests that results in school are increasingly linked to socioeconomic preconditions (Skolverket 2012), i.e. parents' level of education is of greater significance to a student's grades than whether or not the parents have a Swedish or foreign background.

In general, pupils who were born in Sweden and whose parents were also born in Sweden, are more likely to access post-secondary education than pupils born outside of Sweden or with a foreign background (OECD 2017) (OECD, 2016[27]). Immigrant students have higher expectations to complete tertiary education in Sweden (when accounted for socio-economic background and academic performance) than in other OECD countries, though this does not mean that they have the skills to do so (OECD, Forthcoming[28]) In addition, success at school also depends on the age at arrival: gaps in educational outcomes are especially pronounced for immigrant students who have arrived after the age of 12 (OECD, Forthcoming[28]). According to a recent OECD report, almost 38% of migrants between 15 and 24 years of age who had arrived in Sweden after they turned 15 were not in any educational activity. This is the highest figure for OECD countries (OECD 2017).

In 2015, in the city of Gothenburg the gaps in educational attainment between native and foreign born population remained significant. Some 33% of the Swedish-born population in the city had a post-secondary education of three years or more, while this is twice less common among people with a foreign background (23%). People with a migration background who only have primary education are double (21%) of those with a Swedish background (10%) (see Key Statistics). However, the gap between native and foreign born in entering higher education is evening out in Gothenburg: in 2012/13, the percentage of foreign born young adults entering postsecondary education in Gothenburg was 45%, even slightly higher than among youth with a native background (44%). Large variations remain per country of origin, with a higher proportion or tertiary students among those originating from Iran, Bosnia and Iraq and a lower share among youth from Somalia or with Somali background (UKÄ/SCB 2014).

School Segregation issues

According to OECD work (OECD 2010) (OECD, 2015[29]) (OECD, Forthcoming[28]), immigrant children in Sweden often concentrate in certain schools. Gothenburg is no exception, pupils' results are increasingly related to the neighbourhood where the school is located, to socioeconomic conditions and to family background. Parents' freedom of choice of their children's schools might be a factor contributing to school segregation as wealthier parents can choose more high-performing schools for their children, while those options are limited for disadvantaged, immigrant families who mostly choose the schools based on location and availability of financial aid rather than teaching quality (OECD 2017) (OECD, Forthcoming[28]). This is a contentious issue in Sweden, and there are discussions on how to change this situation.

As shown in the investigation of living conditions conducted by the city in 2014 (Gothenburg, 2014[3]): 106), there are large variations in school results between districts, but even larger between different basic units within a same district. In Bergsjön (in the district of Östra Göteborg), a district with a high concentration of population with migration background, only 66% of the girls and 56% of the boys were eligible for secondary schooling in 2013 (see table 7.3), as compared to 100% of the girls and 71 and 82% respectively of the boys (Göteborgs stad 2014: 54) in Kärrdalen/Slättadamm and Norra Älvstranden.[12] However the report also showed that around half of all students who have parents with a low level of education fail to qualify for high school and the level of education of the parents is of greater significance to a student's grades than whether the parents have a Swedish or a foreign background.

Table 5.3. Percentage of pupils eligible for at least vocational secondary education per district

District	Percentage of pupils eligible to at least vocational secondary education
Angered	69.2
East Göteborg	68.9
Örgryte/Härlanda	89.8
Centrum	91.0
Majorna/Linné	87.4
Askim/Frölunda/Högsbo	88.1
Västra Göteborg	87.5
Västra Hisingen	82.3
Lundby	82.8
Norra Hisingen	85.1
Göteborg as a whole	82.2

Source:. Göteborgsbladet 2016.

Some neighbourhoods in Gothenburg are characterised by higher levels of post-secondary education attainment: while in North Angered, only 12% of the population had a post-secondary education of three years or more, the same figure for Stora Sigfridsplan was 51% (Göteborgs stad, 2014: 91).

The large influx of refugees during 2014 and 2015 aggravated the level of school segregation in the city as 15 schools out of a total of 161 in the Greater Gothenburg area bore the brunt of accepting newly arrived children. In those 15 schools, more than 20% of the pupils were newly arrived in 2016. Those 15 schools were situated in the Northeast and in Frölunda/Tynnered (Göteborg direkt 2016). Pupils' concentration in just a few schools is to a certain extent one of the unintended consequences of the fact that asylum seekers organise living conditions by themselves (*egenordnat boende*), which does not encourage a more equitable distribution across districts. The municipality has ranked among its top priorities achieving a more even distribution of newly-arrived students across schools in the city and streamline refugee pupils' reception in preschools and schools (OECD meeting with the municipality, 16 March 2017).

Responses to educational challenges

Access to school:

Since 2013, all children in Sweden between the ages of 6 and 18 have a legal right to attend school, irrespective of their migration status (Education, 2016[25]). Children arriving from other countries[13] are integrated into the national school system, either in primary or secondary schooling, depending on age, with a focus on language learning. Schools have the obligation to assess students' skills within two months after arrival (International, 2017[30]) and the National Agency for Education has the assignment to produce mapping material and assessment material so that schools can measure the pupils' knowledge and skills (Education, 2016[25]). For children enrolled in public schools it is obligatory to participate in regular Swedish classes or Swedish as a second language class. Government grants have also been introduced for extended learning time in Swedish for newly arrived immigrant pupils (Education, 2016[25]). In the upper-secondary school, there are special programmes for newly arrived pupils, but when the language introduction is completed, those pupils join the general classes. All children also have the right to develop both the Swedish language and their mother tongue according to national policies. Education in the mother tongue is offered and is the responsibility of the municipalities.

There are several initiatives from different civil society organisations providing children in primary and secondary schools, in particular students with migration background, with extra support classes and help with their homework and studying. Funding is available for these associations from different local authorities: district authorities, the Social resource management of the municipality and the County Administrative Board.

Measures against school segregation:

As previously indicated by OECD work, municipalities could allocate funding to schools on the basis of multiple indicators – instead of a single indicator – such as the proportion of students with low performance, with parents with low levels of education, and different home language (OECD 2010: 8) (Education, 2016[25]). Increased funding should reduce gaps in the quality of education across schools and potentially attract a more mixed student population. Further according to the Swedish ministry of education incentives should be created so that the best teachers teach in the most challenging schools (Education, 2016[25]). Additionally support could be offered to migrant parents to better orient them when they choose the school for their children. The municipality of Gothenburg is implementing a set of measures against school segregation. For instance it offers advice to parents in who live in socioeconomic poor areas to choose school in another area. Also schools who have a low share of newly arrived need to prioritise enrolment of newcomers over other students.

The situation in Gothenburg presents similarities with the one analysed in the Amsterdam case study, comparative analysis and exchange of practices around this issue could be beneficial for both cities. Municipalities in the Netherlands tried to tackle school selection mechanisms to influence the parental choice system. For instance, some municipalities in the Netherlands (i.e. Nijmegen, etc.) have introduced a central subscription system to assign students to primary schools, in order to reach a share of 30% of disadvantaged students in each school. In other cities (i.e. Rotterdam), crowded schools have been required to give preference to children who would enrich their ethnic and socio-economic mixes.

Learning the language:

Migrant children learn Swedish in school. Language classes for adults are provided within the Swedish for immigrants (sfi) programme. All migrants, regardless of reasons for migrating to Sweden, are eligible to participate in sfi. For newcomers refugees enrolled in the Introduction programme the responsibility for sfi lies with municipalities, which are funded by the central government for 2 years. In the spring of 2017, there was a shortage of sfi teachers in Gothenburg. Municipalities implement the sfi through different stakeholders including non-governmental organisations. For instance, the People's University (*Folkuniversitetet*) is an independent learning institution, specialised in different areas, that is connected with universities. Amongst its offer of adult education courses, funded by the municipality, it provides Swedish for immigrants. Furthermore, the University of Gothenburg has recently started a course in Swedish for newly arrived, in order to enable former university students to meet the language requirements to be eligible for higher education in Sweden.[14]

Studies showed that good knowledge of Swedish increases the likelihood for newcomers to find work and higher pay. However, several studies have concluded that the education in SFI is not working as intended (DELMI, 2017[15]).

Access to Higher education:

In order to facilitate paths to higher education, or work in the academic sector, for young newcomers the municipality of Gothenburg, the county government and the Västra Götaland region cooperate with the University of Gothenburg and the Employment Agency. These initiatives target newcomers with aspirations to proceed into tertiary education: prior students with interrupted university studies or university teachers and scholars wishing to continue to pursue an academic career. Cooperation occurs through joint activities such as: providing for internships, Summer school for refugees, and information meetings for newly arrived individuals with an interest in higher education.

Adult complementary and vocational education:

The Swedish adult education system, which also applies to individuals who would be ineligible for university training, offers a large variety of measures for adult migrants and newly arrived individuals so they can improve their qualification. Some of those opportunities are universal adult education offered to all persons in need to fill in gaps in secondary education: complementary education, adult education, vocational education, etc. This flexibility was particularly needed given the diversity of profiles of the newcomers. In terms of educational attainment among the new arrivals in recent years, there is a contradictory pattern. In 2014, over 30% of humanitarian migrants arriving in Sweden held some form of tertiary degree, while others bring only very basic levels of education and . In the same year, 37% of humanitarian migrants held only a primary or lower-secondary education (OECD, 2016[11]).

One example of post-secondary vocational education accessible to the general public, is called Higher Vocational Education, with several hundred different programmes and designed to fit competence needs in the labour market. In 2010, 20% of those who initiated studies within the Higher Vocational Education were of foreign origin (Myndigheten för yrkeshögskolan 2011). The Higher Vocational Education is organised by different actors, for example private educational companies, municipalities, counties or universities/colleges. The National Agency of Higher Vocational Education must grant validation for each programme.

One rather specific form of adult education provided by organisations, foundations or NGOs is called ''folk high school'' (*folkhögskola*). The Västra Götaland region runs and finances six such schools, including Gothenburg's folk high school. Their intention is to fill in deficiencies in secondary education, or provide opportunities in new directions for individuals, who are experiencing schooling delays or are past the schooling age. Often, they are organised as boarding schools.

Complementary (supplementary or bridging) education has existed in Sweden since the 1990s (DELMI, 2017[15]) and targets foreigners who are registered in Sweden and have a professional qualification from a tertiary education institution in her/his country of origin. In fact previous evaluations had indicated that the validation of professional qualifications (see paragraph below) worked better if accompanied by extra training at school or at the workplace. People who completed these courses are more likely to find work. Chances are higher for those with a specific vocational college or university degree rather than general degree (DELMI, 2017[15]). Complementary education is organised by universities and offered in regulated professions that require some kind of licence or registration to work in that field (for example health professions, lawyers, veterinarians, economics, psychology, biomedical scientists, dentist, electricians, security guards and social workers). For example, complementary education in health professions is targeted towards non-EU citizens who hold a degree in medicine.

In 2016, the Fast Track initiative was introduced by the Swedish government and offered to skilled immigrants with qualifications in shortage occupations (20 professions have been identified including: pharmacists, dentists, nurses, physicians, teachers, etc.) complementary education in their mother tongue. The decision to provide education in migrants' mother tongue for specific occupations recognises that language requirements should not be a reason for delaying migrants, particularly skilled ones, from entering the labour market (OECD, 2016[11]). This is in line with the consensus during OECD interviews in Gothenburg with private sector representatives who are ready to accept migrants who only speak English for professions where there are labour shortages (i.e. construction, engineering sectors, etc.). Newly arrived individuals receive information about Fast Track and recognition opportunities within the establishment programme. For instance, a fast track course for teachers is offered in Gothenburg, where parts of the education are offered in Arabic. Also, the Småland Blekinge region implemented in 2017 a "fast track for health professionals" programme, which validates foreign exams and competencies (OECD, Monitor of Smaland Bleking review 2018, forthcoming). In particular, the Kalmar county council, which is responsible for publicly-funded health care, has a "fast track" for validation to absorb refugees with professional training in health care as doctors, nurses, pharmacists, laboratory personnel, dentists, (Sveriges Kommuner och Landsting, 2018[27]) . They scout out the newly arrived individuals long before they receive their permit of residence and schedule training, internship, validation and other assistance in order to speed up the legal process. In addition, Emmaboda municipality in Kalmar county is leading a project called "Ny resurs" (New resource) to support refugees and other newly arrived individuals with a university degree or similar training (Ny resurs, 2018[26]).

Assessment and recognition of foreign qualifications:

Validation of competence has been included in Sweden integration policy since the early 2000s (DELMI, 2017[15]). Foreign education is validated by a national authority, the Swedish Council for Higher Education (UHR) created in 2013. This serves as one-stop-shop for all types of qualifications and is responsible for the assessment and recognition of foreign upper-secondary, post-secondary, and tertiary education for labour market purposes in unregulated professions and for teachers. Information about recognition procedure is part of the regular introduction scheme for newly arrived migrants (OECD, Making integration work: assessment and recognition of foreign qualifications, 2017).

Box 5.1. Regional association's efforts to enhance diploma recognition

Together with four other sub-regional associations and the Region, the Gothenburg Regional Association set up an organisation called Validering Väst (Validation West). This organisation works with various stakeholders (including the Employment agency) in order to help individuals receive documented proof of their skills (e.g. as an electrician or a builder, etc.) so that they can work in specific professions that require a license or formal education -to be released by Swedish Council for Higher Education (UHR)-. One of their goals for 2017 is to create conditions so that newcomers to Sweden can have their practical skills "made visible" and documented.

Notes

[1] As described before this is special support offered to refugees, resettled refugees, in need of protection or relatives of any of these individuals who have received a residence permit between 20-64 years of age. Persons between 18 and 20 without parents in Sweden are also entitled to these activities. Participation is voluntary and the person needs to register with the Swedish Tax Agency to obtain a personal identity number in order to enrol.

[2] Introduction act (http://www.notisum.se/rnp/sls/lag/20100197.htm)

[3] During this time, beneficiaries receive the introduction benefit, which consists of the same package across the country, and is contingent on attendance of the activities. On average, the benefit provides €33 (SEK 308) per working day, and up to a maximum additional SEK 4 500 per month for those with children.

[4] Labour market policies and the responsibility of assisting people struggling to find a job lie with the Public Employment Service Arbetsförmedlingen (PES), a central government authority. Local PES offices are present throughout the country: people already living in Sweden, with a work or resident permit, can register as a jobseeker. PES offices can offer a variety of tools and advice to help jobseekers find work.

[5] An interpreter is usually available.

[6] As part of the municipal welfare services, municipalities are responsible for the labour market integration of most vulnerable groups (i.e. unemployed with only pre-secondary education, born outside Europe, aged 55-64 years, reduced working abilities, etc.).

[7] https://www.businessregiongoteborg.se/en/about-us.

[8] .http://www.grkom.se/toppmenyn/dettajobbargrmed/miljoochsamhallsbyggnad/projekt/kompetens matchningsmodellen/parattplats.4.38eb075115f4e76ea5b3059.html

[9] In 2016, 830 newly arrived individuals and unaccompanied asylum-seeking minors were accommodated. Some 500 were offered sublease contracts through the public housing companies and 150 were staying in mobile camping vans at Lilleby campground. Another 100 stayed in other temporary and preliminary premises including rented accommodations from private actors. Around 80 persons were staying in dormitories. In addition, some residents in Torslanda engaged in the reception process and developed contacts between residents and newly arrived individuals (Additional information provided by the City Executive Office, 9 May 2017).

[10] https://www.1177.se/Vastra-Gotaland/Regler-och-rattigheter/Vard-av-personer-fran-andra-lander1/

[11] https://www.1177.se/Vastra-Gotaland/Other-languages/Engelska/Regler-och-rattigheter/Vard-i-Sverige-om-man-ar-asylsokande-gomd-eller-papperslos/

[12] There are in general in Sweden large variations between boys and girls when it comes to school results.

[13] For children arriving from EU/EEA countries who stay less than three months municipalities don't have the obligation to provide them with schooling but Gothenburg offer them access to their schools.

[14] Applicants must have strong Swedish and English language skills in order to be accepted to university.

Bibliography

Andersson, R. (2010), *Contextualising ethnic residential segregation in Sweden: welfare, housing and migration-related policies.* [14]

Arbetsformedlingen (2016), *Living and Working in Sweden.* [13]

Bakbasel (2012), *Migration: attractiveness, openness, integration. An international benchmarking for Goteborg and Vastsverige.* [5]

Blanchenay, P., T. Burns and F. Köster (2014), "Shifting Responsibilities - 20 Years of Education Devolution in Sweden: A Governing Complex Education Systems Case Study", *OECD Education Working Papers*, No. 104, OECD Publishing, Paris, http://dx.doi.org/10.1787/5jz2jg1rqrd7-en. [24]

DELMI (2017), *The pathway to work – foreign-born people's encounter with the Swedish labour market.* [15]

Education, S. (2016), *OECD School resources review: Sweden*, OECD Publishing, http://www.oecd.org/education/school/CBR_OECD_SRR_SE-FINAL.pdf. [25]

Emilsson (2015), "A national turn of local integration policy: multi-level governance dynamics in Denmark and Sweden", *Comparative Migration Studies*, Vol. 3/1, p. 7. [18]

European Commission (2017), *Fast Track Initiative for newly arrived immigrants*, European Commission. [6]

Fratzke, S. (2017), *Weathering Crisis Forging Ahead: Swedish asylum and integration policy*, Migration Policy Institute. [20]

Gothenburg, C. (2014), *Report on inequality in living conditions and health in Gothenburg. A socially sustainable city*, City of Gothenburg. [3]

International, E. (2017), *Newcomers Hope in a cold climate*, Education International. [30]

Migration, S. (2017), *Satatistics persons with accommodation in the Swedish Migration Agency's reception system.* [31]

OECD/UCLG (2016), *Subnational Governments around the world: structure and finance*, OECD/UCLG. [10]

OECD (2014), *Effective public investment across levels of government. Principles for action*, https://www.oecd.org/effective-public-investment-toolkit/Effective-Public-Investment-Brochure.pdf. [16]

OECD (2015), *Improving Schools in Sweden: An OECD Perspective*, OECD Publishing, http://www.oecd.org/education/school/Improving-Schools-in-Sweden.pdf. [26]

OECD (2015), *Immigrant Students at School: Easing the Journey towards Integration*, OECD [29]

Publishing.

OECD (2016), *Working Together: Skills and Labour Market Integration of Immigrants and their children in Sweden*, OECD Publishing http://dx.doi.org/10.1787/9789264257382-en. [11]

OECD (2016), *OECD Better Policies series:, Promoting Well-being and Inclusiveness in Sweden*, OECD Publishing, http://dx.doi.org/10.1787/9789264259980-en. [4]

OECD (2016), *How's Life in the Netherlands*, OECD. [7]

OECD (2016), *OECD Regional Outlook 2016: productive regions for inclusive societies*, OECD Publisher. [22]

OECD (2016), *PISA 2015 Results (Volume I): Excellence and Equity in Education, PISA,*, OECD Publishing, Paris.. [27]

OECD (2016b), *Making Integration Work*, OECD. [2]

OECD (2017), *International Migration Outlook*, OECD Publishing. [8]

OECD (2017), *Territorial review Sweden*, OECD Publisher. [9]

OECD (2017), *Land use planning systems in the OECD: country fact sheets*, OECD Publisher. [17]

OECD (2017), *Country profile – Sweden. Multilevel governance of public investment*, https://www.oecd.org/effective-public-investment-toolkit/Sweden.pdf. [19]

OECD (2017a), *OECD Territorial Reviews: Sweden 2017: Monitoring Progress in Multi-level Governance and Rural Policy*, OECD Publishing. [23]

OECD (2018), *Working together for integration of migrants and refugees at the local level*, OECD Publishing. [1]

OECD (Forthcoming), *The resilience of students with an immigrant background: factors that shape well-being*, OECD Publishing. [28]

Regerungskansliet (2009), *Swedish Integration Policy*, Ministry of Integration and Gender Equality. [12]

Swedish Migration agency (2017), *Swedish Resettlement programme*. [21]

Further readings

Aldén, Lina & Mats Hammarstedt, 2017, *Egenföretagande bland utrikesfödda: En översikt av utvecklingen under 2000-talet*, Arbetsmarknadsekonomiska rådet, underlagsrapport 1/2017.

Andersson Joona, Pernilla; Alma Wennemo Lanninger & Marianne Sundström, 2016, *Etableringsreformens effekter på de nyanländas integration. Slutrapport*, Stockholms universitets Linnécenter för integration

Andersson, Roger et al, 2009, *Fattiga och rika—segregerad stad*, Göteborgs stad.

Arbetsförmedlingen, 2017, *Var finns jobben? Bedömning för 2017*, https://www.arbetsformedlingen.se/download/18.40fa4e7b159ff02933130b86/1486626381471/Var-finns-jobben-2017.pdf

Arbetsförmedlingen, 2017, *Perspektiv på arbetslösheten i olika grupper*, https://www.arbetsformedlingen.se/download/18.35e8e8ea159c5a24b2c54862/1485872614435/Perspektiv_pa_arbetslosheten_i_olika_grupper_korr.pdf

Arbetsmarknadsekonomiska rådet, 2017, *Tudelningarna på arbetsmarknaden*.

BRÅ, Brottsförebyggande rådet, 2016; *Hatbrott 2015; Statistik över polisanmälningar med identifierade hatbrottsmotiv och självrapporterat utsatthet för hatbrott.* Rapport 2016:15, Stockholm.

Business Region Göteborg, 2016, Skandinaviens mest expansiva region: 100 % fakta och statistic om Göteborgsregionens näringsliv 2016.

Castles, Stephen, Hein de Haas and Mark Miller (eds), 2013, *The Age of Migration, Fifth Edition: International Population Movements in the Modern World*, Palgrave.

Dagens Medicin, 2016, https://www.dagensmedicin.se/artiklar/2016/04/15/okunskap-om-papperslosas-ratt-i-varden/.

Demker, Marie & Sara van der Meiden, 2016, ''Allt starkare polarisering och allt lägre flyktingmotstånd'', i Ohlsson, Oscarsson & Solevid (red), pp.197–2014.

Diedrich, Andreas & Alexander Styhre, 2013, ''Constructing the employable immigrant: The uses of validation practices in Sweden'', *ephemera:theory & politics in organization*, Vol 13(4): 759–783

Ds 2016:37, Åldersbedömning tidigare i asylprocessen, http://www.regeringen.se/4a75cf/contentassets/bbc0c954e356474e9dfbbf021d94afbf/aldersbedomnin g-tidigare-i-asylprocessen-ds-201637

DO (Diskrimineringsombudsmannen), 2014, *Forskningsöversikt om rekrytering i arbetslivet: Forskning som publicerats vid svenska universitet och högskolor sedan 2000*, Oxford Research Group.

DO (Diskrimineringsombudsmannen), 2016, *Kedjor av händelser: En analys av anmälningar om diskriminering från muslimer och förmodade muslimer*

Eastmond, Marita, 2011,"Egalitarian Ambitions, Constructions of Difference: The Paradoxes of Refugee Integration in Sweden" i *Journal of Ethnic and Migration Studies*, 37 (pp. 277-295)

Evidens, 2016, *Trångboddhet i Sverige—beskrivning av nuläget och diskussion om effekter.*

Expo, 2016, *Stängda dörrar.*

Forkby, Torbjörn och Susanne Liljeholm Hansson, 2011: *Kampen för att bli någon: Bilder av förorten och riskfyllda utvecklingsvägar i Göteborg*; FoU i Väst, Rapport 1: 2011.

GP, 2016, http://www.gp.se/nyheter/göteborg/så-mycket-extra-asylpengar-får-stadsdelarna-1.3922.

GP, 2017, https://www.gp.se/nyheter/göteborg/nu-vill-kommunen-inte-hyra-tillfälliga-bostäder-i-frihamnen-längre-1.4218509.

Göteborgsbladet, 2016, *Områdesfakta*, Samhällsanalys och Statistik, Göteborgs stadsledningskontor.

Göteborg direkt, 2016, http://www.goteborgdirekt.se/nyheter/har-ar-skolorna-som-tar-emot-goteborgs-nyanlanda/reppjl!TXem5kqTYcD@DGGcYleiKg/

Göteborgsregionens kommunalförbund, 2015, *Flyktingmottagandet i Göteborgsregionen: en återrapport*, Dnr15-232.60

Göteborgs stad, 2013, *Rätt boende 2012–2015: En socialt hållbar stad—ett sammanhållet Göteborg. Strategi bostadsförsörjning för nyanlända flyktingar.*

Göteborgs stad, 2014, *Skillnader i livsvillkor och hälsa i Göteborg,*

Göteborgs stad: Stadsledningskontoret, 2015, *Åtgärder för effektivare mottagning och säkerställande av boendeplatser för ensamkommande barn*, Dnr 1378/15

Göteborgs stad, 2016, *Stadens hantering av bosättningsprocess för nyanlända som anvisas av Arbetsförmedlingen alternativt Migrationsverket enligt lag (SFS 2016: 38) om mottagning av visa nyanlända invandrare för bosättning*, Dnr1616/15

Joyce, P. (2015) "Integrationspolitik och arbetsmarknad" Delegation for migration studies (DELMI) 2015:3, Ministry of Justice, Sweden.

Joyce, P. (2017) "Inspiration för Integration" Report to the Expert group on public economics (ESO) 2017:7, Ministry of Finance, Sweden.

Hussein, Jamila, 2014, *Kulturföreningar i nordöstra Göteborg: En utredning gjord av Jamila Hussein 2011–2013*, Göteborgs stad; Utveckling nordost.

Lag (1994: 137) om mottagning av asylsökande m fl (http://www.riksdagen.se/sv/dokument-lagar/dokument/svensk-forfattningssamling/lag-1994137-om-mottagande-av-asylsokande-mfl_sfs-1994-137).

Lag (2016:752) om tillfälliga begränsningar av möjligheten att få uppehållstillstånd i Sverige; https://www.riksdagen.se/sv/dokument-lagar/dokument/svensk-forfattningssamling/lag-2016752-om-tillfalliga-begransningar-av_sfs-2016-752

Lag (2010: 197); Lag om etableringsinsatser för visa nyanlända; https://www.riksdagen.se/sv/dokument-lagar/dokument/svensk-forfattningssamling/lag-2010197-om-etableringsinsatser-for-vissa_sfs-2010-197.

Larsson, Göran & Mårten Björk, 2015, *Globala konflikter med lokala konsekvenser: översikt om utresandeproblematiken*, Myndigheten för samhällsskydd och beredskap.

Lindbäck, Jonas; Johannes Lunneblad & Ove Sernhede, 2016: *Skolan och den territoriella stigmatiseringen—Om två skolor i den urbana periferin*, i *Educare*, Malmö högskola, 2016: 1, pp. 110–130.

Lindholm Schulz, Helena, 2003, *The Palestinian Diaspora: Formation of Identities and Politics of Homeland*, Routledge.

Länsstyrelsen 2017; http://extra.lansstyrelsen.se/integration/Sv/tidiga-insatser-asylsokande/Sidor/default.aspx.

Migrationsinfo, 2016, ''Papperslösa'', http://www.migrationsinfo.se/migration/sverige/papperslosa/, entered 28 February 2017.

Migrationsverket – Swedish Migration Board (2014), "Systemanalys av asylprocessen – en analys av ett komplext system utifrån en systemansats, delrapport" [System analysis of the asylum process – An analysis of a complex system based on a systems approach, progress report], Migrationsverket, Stockholm.

Migrationsverket, 2016, Årsredovisning, https://www.migrationsverket.se/download/18.4100dc0b159d67dc6142a4e/1487775100129/Årsredovisning+2016.pdf

Migrationsverket, 2017, *Verksamhets- och utgiftsprognos*, https://www.migrationsverket.se/download/18.4100dc0b159d67dc614b0d/1486539367565/Migrationsverkets+prognos+2017_febr+P2-17.pdf

Myndigheten för yrkeshögskolan, 2011, https://www.myh.se/Nyhetsrum/Pressmeddelanden/2011/Var-femte-studerande-pa-yrkeshogskolan-har-utlandsk-bakgrund/.

OECD 2010, OECD Reviews of Migrant Education - Closing the Gap for Immigrant Students: Policies, Practice and Performance – Country Review Sweden

OECD, 2015, Income Inequality Data Update: Sweden (January 2015)

OECD (2016) OECD Better Policies series: *Promoting Well-being and Inclusiveness in Sweden*, OECD Publishing, Paris, http://dx.doi.org/10.1787/9789264259980-en

OECD (2017) OECD Territorial Reviews: Sweden 2017: Monitoring Progress in Multi-level Governance and Rural Policy, OECD Publishing Paris

OECD (2016), *Working Together: Skills and Labour Market Integration of Immigrants and their Children in Sweden*, OECD Publishing, Paris, http://dx.doi.org/10.1787/9789264257382-en.

OECD (2015) *How's Life? 2015: Measuring Well-being*, OECD Publishing, Paris, http://dx.doi.org/10.1787/how_life-2015-en.

OECD (2015), *Improving Schools in Sweden: An OECD Perspective*, OECD Publishing, Paris, http://www.oecd.org/edu/school/improving-schools-in-sweden-an-oecd-perspective.htm.

OECD (2015), *Employment and Skills Strategies in Sweden*, OECD Reviews on Local Job Creation, OECD Publishing, Paris, http://dx.doi.org/10.1787/9789264228641-en.

OECD (2015d), *Education at a Glance*, OECD Publishing, Paris, http://dx.doi.org/10.1787/eag-2015-en.

OECD (2014), PISA 2012 Results: What Students Know and Can Do (Volume I, Revised edition, February 2014): Student Performance in Mathematics, Reading and Science, PISA, OECD Publishing, Paris, http://dx.doi.org/10.1787/9789264208780-en.

OECD (2014) Recommendation of the Council on Effective Public Investment Across Levels of Government, http://www.oecd.org/gov/regional-policy/recommendation-effective-public-investment-across-levels-of-government.htm.

Ohlsson Jonas, Henrik Oscarsson & Maria Solevid (red), 2016, *Ekvilibrium*, SOM-undersökningen 2015; SOM-rapport nr 66.

Olwog, Karen Fog, 2011, ''Integration'': Migrants and Refugees between Scandinavian Welfare Societies and Family Relations'', in *Journal of Ethnic and Migration Studies*, Vol. 37, No. 2.

Polisen, 2015, *Utsatta områden: Sociala risker, kollektiv förmåga och oönskade händelser*, Nationella operative avdelningen, Underrättelseenheten.

Polisen & Göteborgs stad, 2017, *Särskilt utsatta områden i Göteborg; Analys av rapporterna ''Utsatta områden—sociala risker, kollektiv förmåga och oänskade händelser samt ''Skillnader i livsvillkor och hälsa i Göteborg''*, authored by Nakisha Khorramshahi & Stefan Hellberg.

Portes, Alejandro, 1999 ''Conclusion: Towards a New World—The Origins and Effects of Transnational Activities'', *Ethnic and Racial Studies*, Vol. 22, No. 2, March 1999, pp. 463–477.

Riksdagen, 2016, https://www.riksdagen.se/sv/dokument-lagar/dokument/svensk-forfattningssamling/lag-201638-om-mottagande-av-vissa-nyanlanda_sfs-2016-38).

Scocco, Sandro & Lars Fredrik Andersson, 2015, *900 miljarder skäl att uppskatta invandring: En analys av invandringens effekter på de offentliga finansierna i Sverige 1950–2014*, Arena Idé.

Skolverket, 2012, *Likvärdig utbildning i svensk grundskola? En kvantitativ analys av likvärdighet över tid.* Rapport nr 374.

SOM 2017, http://som.gu.se/aktuellt/Nyheter/Nyheter_detalj//resultat-fran-som-seminariet-2017.cid1440889.

Statistiska centralbyrån, 2016–2017; Statistical material (http://www.scb.se)

Statistiska centralbyrån, 2015, *Vilka valde att välja? Deltagandet i valet 2014*, Demokratistatistik: Rapport 19.

Statistiska centralbyrån, 2016, http://www.scb.se/sv_/Hitta-statistik/Statistik-efter-amne/Arbetsmarknad/Arbetskraftsundersokningar/Arbetskraftsundersokningarna-AKU/23265/23272/Behallare-for-Press/399739/.

Strömbäck, Jesper, 2016: *Utan invandring stannar Sverige*, Volante.

Sveriges advokatsamund, 2017, https://www.advokatsamfundet.se/globalassets/advokatsamfundet_sv/nyheter/brev-fran-sveiges-advokatsamfund-till-mikael-ribbenvik-rorande-medicinska-aldersbedomningar-.pdf

SvT, 2017a, http://www.svt.se/nyheter/lokalt/vast/flera-sjalvmord-bland-ensamkommande.

SvT, 2017b, (http://www.svt.se/nyheter/inrikes/244-000-fler-i-arbete-alla-utrikesfodda?cmpid=del%3Apd%3Any%3A20170327%3A244-000-fler-i-arbete-alla-utrikesfodda%3Anyh)

SvT, 2017c, (http://www.svt.se/nyheter/lokalt/vast/over-90-anlagda-brander-pa-asylboenden-forra-aret)

Sweco, 2015, *Etableringsgrad.*

Sydsvenskan, 2016, http://www.sydsvenskan.se/2016-10-01/farre-eu-migranter-i-sverige-infor-vintern.

Törnquist, Anders, 2005, *Allting förändras, men ingenting förgås*; Summerande utvärdering av Storstadssatsningen i Göteborg.

Vertovec, Steven, 1999 'Conceiving and Researching Transnationalism', *Ethnic and Racial Studies,* Vol. 22, No. 2, March 1999., pp. 447– 462,

Västra Götalandsregionen, 2017, *Arbetsmarknadsprognos för vanligaste yrken i Västra Götaland,* http://www.vgregion.se/upload/Regionutveckling/Publikationer/2015/yrkesbarometer%20vanliga%20 jobb%20Västra%20Götaland.pdf

UKÄ/SCB, 2014, *Universitet och högskolor: svensk och utländsk bakgrund för studenter och doktorander 2012/13.*

Web-links

https://www.1177.se/Vastra-Gotaland/Other-languages/Engelska/Regler-och-rattigheter/Vard-Sverige-om-man-ar-asylsokande-gomd-eller-papperslos/.
http://www.esf.se/Min-region/Vastsverige/Utlysningar/Kommande-utlysningar/.
http://socialutveckling.goteborg.se/team/brottsforebyggande-arbete/trygg-i-goteborg.
http://www.valideringvast.se/om-oss/.

Annex A: List of participants in the meetings held in Gothenburg with the OECD-team 15–17 March 2017

Civil society organisations, 15 March 2017, in the offices of Västra Götaland region

- Bilal Almobarak, Gothenburg branch coordinator of the Support Group Network
- Mohad Aruqi, Development officer, Social inclusion department, Red Cross
- My Barkensjö, Registered Nurse, Member of the board, Rosengrenska
- Malin Breitner, Head of Desk, Regional development, Red Cross
- Adnan Abdul Ghani, Project Manager (Save the Children), initiator Support Group Network
- Gun Holmertz, Operational Manager, Caritas
- Madlin Krabit, Assistant, Volunteer Center, Caritas
- Gudrun Romeborn, Agape
- Matti Wirehag, Vice chairperson, Rosengrensa
- Representative, Individual människorhjälp
- *The municipality: policy: 16 March in the City Hall*
- Ann-Sofie Hermansson, Chairwoman of Gothenburg municipal board,
- Marina Johansson, City Councellor, social issues including refugee reception Head of Social Resource committe
- Henrik Ripa, City Councellor, Lerum municipality
- *Initial reception, 16 March 2017, in the City Hall*
- Talieh Ashjari, Head of Unit Social Sustainability, County Government
- Pia Borg, Planning leader, Migration and integration, Gothenburg Municipality Executive Office
- Helene Holmström, Operational Director, Integration, Gothenburg Municipality, Social Resource Management
- Sven Höper, Director for welfare and education, Gothenburg Municipality Executive Office
- Oskar Johansson, Coordinator, County Government
- Marcus Toremar, Head of Region West, National Migration Agency

Housing, 16 March, in the Gothenburg City Hall

- Anna Bengtsson, Project leader , Gothenburg Municipality, City Planning
- Erik Gedeck, Head of Unit, Gothenburg Municipality, Real Estate Office
- Tobias Johansson, Head of Sustainability, FutureConcern Ltd
- Kristian Käll, Process leader, social sustainability, Älvstranden Development Ltd

Education, 16 March 2017, at the Integration Centre

- Sarah Males, School principal, Education committee
- Helen Svelid, Planning leader education, Gothenburg Municipality, Executive Office

Health, 16 March 2017, at the Integration Centre

- Henry Ascher, MD, Professor in Public Health, Assoc. professor in Paediatrics - University of Gothenburg Consultant and Clinician - Angered Hospital and The Child Refugee Team
- Lina Gustin, Project leader "Hälsa i Sverige för asylsökande och nyanlända", Västra Götaland region, healthcare
- Britt Tallhage, Executive Manager, Crisis and Trauma Clinic

Youth, risk and social inclusion

- Ulf Boström, Integration police officer, The Police
- Magnus Bergström, Social worker, social welfare office
- Gunilla Hemmingson, Development Manager, Safety promotion and crime prevention issues, Gothenburg Municipality
- Daniel Hjerpe, Coordinator, The Police
- Even Magnusson, Crime Prevention, The Police

Labour-market and adult education, 16 March 2017, at the Integration Office

- Stefan Gustavsson, Director of Industrial Policy, West Swedish Chamber of Commerce
- Sanaz Haghghi, Establishment administrator, National Employment Agency
- Björn Dufva Hellsten, Validation West
- Peter Karanschi, EURES adviser,
- Johan Roos, Head of adult education, Swedish for Immigrants, Adult Education
- Lena Westling-Seliee, Section Manager, Establishment Unit, National Employment Agency
- Ulf Wallin, Adult education, National Employment Agency

Integration Centre, 16 March 2017, at the Integration Centre

- Tomas Magnusson, Head of Unit, Integration Centre
- *District Angered, 17 March, in Blå Stället, Angered*
- Kajsa Ahlström, Public health coordinator, Gothenburg Municipality, district committee Angered
- Andreas Johansson, Mentor SOS Children's Villagers
- Sufyan Kadhim, Head of Unit, Angeredskompassen, Gothenburg Municipality, district committee Angered
- Emma Sköld, Mentor SOS Children's Villagers
- Focus Group with four inhabitants in Angered, two young refugee girls (one from Iraq, one from Kurdistan/Syria), one teenage girl from Colombia, one woman from Syria
- Additional information provided by the City Executive Office, 9 and 27 May 2017.
- Additional information provided by the Västra Götaland region 22 May 2017.

Annex B: Division of competences for integration relevant matters across levels of government

NATIONAL: no national "integration code" or guidelines, integration is mainstreamed in general policies		
Entity	**Responsible for/Past capacities**	**Important updates in competences/legislation**
Integration Agency	created in 1997 and dismantled in 2007	
Ministry of Justice - Swedish Migration Agency	- Immediate reception - handling the asylum seeking process from registration through management to decision, - accommodation of all asylum seekers - since January 2017 is responsible for *assigning municipality places for newly arrived persons with a resident status, including resettled refugees.*	A new Asylum law (2016:752) was introduced in July 2016: limiting residence permits for refugees to three years and for those holding a subsidiary protection status to 13 months. After this limit if there are still reasons for protection, a prolonged permit may be granted. If the person is able to supply for her-/himself, a permanent permit of residence may be granted. Possibilities for family reunification are exceptional for those entitled with subsidiary protection. Since the introduction of the Reception for Settlement Act (2016:38) in March 2016 the Swedish Migration Agency became responsible for *assigning municipality places for newly arrived persons* with residence permits including resettled refugees, taking over this role from the Employment agency. Before the agency was responsible only to finding housing to quota refugees, elderly and those refugees who are unable to participate in the establishment programme due to disabilities
Ministry of Employment	Employment, establishment, integration through work	
Equality Ombudsman (DO)	Overseeing discrimination laws	A comprehensive law against all kinds of discrimination was introduced in 2009
Public Employment Service (PES) *Arbetsformedlingen* **– under the authority of the Ministry of Employment**	Introduction programme	Until 2010 municipalities were responsible for this programme.
Regional Authorities		
Västra Götalandsregionen - County Council Elected regional body	Doesn't have appointed tasks related to integration but is actively involved in facilitating the establishment of newcomers and has a large responsibility when it comes to health care	Collaborates with the county government in the implementation of Early initiatives.
County governments (Länsstyrelsen) Deconcentrated national administration	Support the municipalities in receiving unaccompanied children, coordinating educational activities in Swedish and societal orientation. They distribute state grants for reception and housing to municipalities	From January 2017 they are responsible for "Early initiatives" for asylum seekers
Larger Gothenburg		
Gothenburg Regional Association	Through the association 13 municipalities coordinated on issues related to infrastructure, traffic, pollution, etc.	Since 2015 peak in refugee arrivals they extended their cooperation on issues related to housing and integrating newcomers
MUNICIPAL: integration is a responsibility for all municipal boards and is mainstreamed in municipal policies as a whole and is not the responsibility of an integration department but		

Entity	Responsible for/Past capacities	Important updates in competences/legislation
Municipality	Housing and education	Within the framework of the Introduction programme municipalities are in charge of Swedish classes, housing, and initiatives for children in schools and pre-school as well as civic orientation services.
Interpreter and migrant service and Special Board for migrant issues	Created in 1970-80 and phased out in 2000 when the activities were transferred to other municipal boards	
Advisor on migration, integration and refugee reception in the City executive office	This role contributes to reaching consensus and a holistic view of the political orientations of the city in this domain	
Management group for receiving and integrating new arrivals	Heads of units of different municipal boards (housing, education and labour market, social affairs) regularly participate to this group. The aim is to make the reception and integration of newly arrived individuals as effective and smooth as possible, through a shared action plan.	
Participation	Right to vote and be voted to municipal elections for all foreigners who lived in the city for more than 3 years	

Source: Author elaboration.

ORGANISATION FOR ECONOMIC CO-OPERATION AND DEVELOPMENT

The OECD is a unique forum where governments work together to address the economic, social and environmental challenges of globalisation. The OECD is also at the forefront of efforts to understand and to help governments respond to new developments and concerns, such as corporate governance, the information economy and the challenges of an ageing population. The Organisation provides a setting where governments can compare policy experiences, seek answers to common problems, identify good practice and work to co-ordinate domestic and international policies.

The OECD member countries are: Australia, Austria, Belgium, Canada, Chile, the Czech Republic, Denmark, Estonia, Finland, France, Germany, Greece, Hungary, Iceland, Ireland, Israel, Italy, Japan, Korea, Latvia, Luxembourg, Mexico, the Netherlands, New Zealand, Norway, Poland, Portugal, the Slovak Republic, Slovenia, Spain, Sweden, Switzerland, Turkey, the United Kingdom and the United States. The European Union takes part in the work of the OECD.

OECD Publishing disseminates widely the results of the Organisation's statistics gathering and research on economic, social and environmental issues, as well as the conventions, guidelines and standards agreed by its members.

OECD PUBLISHING, 2, rue André-Pascal, 75775 PARIS CEDEX 16
(85 2018 09 1 P) ISBN 978-92-64-29959-7 – 2018